Absolutely
THE ∧CRITICAL
NON-ÊSSENTIALS®

How business inessentials give
customers a deep appreciation of the
value you give to them ... and a 'great
business' story to tell their friends!

Happiness & Profit: The Paddi Series...

... of business books and training publications
  Building the Happiness-Centred Business
  The Absolutely Critical Non-Essentials
  Training Customers to Treasure Your Business
  The Secret of Customers Who Love to Pay
  Simply Stunning Customer Service
  Mobilising Your Customer Sales Force

Plus other practical kits and training programs...
  The Welcome Book Construction Kit
  The Courtesy System Tool-Kit
  Courtesy System Action Plaques
  The Original Paddi Story – Audio Recordings
  The Complete Paddi Story – Video Recordings
  The Ultimate Paddi Story – Video Recordings

© Solutions Press, 1996-2006.
  Telephone: (+61-7) 3823 3230
  Facsimile: (+61-7) 3390 3610
  E-mail: info@solutionspress.com.au
  http://www.solutionspress.com.au

SOLUTIONS PRESS BUSINESS PUBLISHING
149 Old Cleveland Road, Capalaba, Queensland, Australia 4157

II

CONTENTS

APPRECIATION

I would like to thank:

My mother and father who gave me a long term-big picture view of my life.

My tutors at dental school and Mr Selwyn at Nottingham Maxillo-facial Unit, who gave me an appreciation of the importance of attention-to-detail.

My friend George, who showed me that there was power in hospitality and the seemingly non-essentials, even in a hard business world.

Fletcher, who has challenged, prodded and encouraged me for the last ten years.

Pat, Merilyn and Annette who put up with my typing when they knew I should have been seeing my next client.

Clive Woodward, who elevated CNe's to a new level.

Paul Dunn, who believed in my crazy ideas.

My children Kate and Sarah, who taught me to be humble.

Ronald Philip and Thomas, who showed me that blood was not thicker than water.

And last but far from least, the ladies in my life — Wendy, Debra and Tracey — who helped civilise me.

PREAMBLE

Michael Hawker, CEO, Insurance Australia Group.

I first came across the name, Paddi Lund, through my very good friend Clive Woodward, who lives in the UK. He told me I should read Paddi's first book, *Building the Happiness-Centred Business*, which he had been given by a prominent US based entrepreneur.

I became more intrigued when he told me that the book was the best customer service book he had ever read, and that the book was written by an Australian dentist, no less, from Capalaba (a satellite suburb of Brisbane).

What my friend liked most about Paddi was the way he paid so much attention to his customers and all the details of their experience.

For many people going to the dentist can be a nightmare, so Paddi put TV's on the ceiling, put 'pain buzzers' in patients hands to alert him when to stop. He began serving a selection of dozens of teas and freshly ground coffees in Royal Doulton fine bone china and silver tea service. He served fresh baked 'dental buns' to his clients in well appointed individual 'personal lounges' with clients' names and photographs on the door.

Paddi didn't like dealing with so many ungrateful patients, so he took down all his signs, removed his name from the phone book and locked his front door. He then 'fired' 75% of his patients and now only works with a small number of high quality, highly enjoyable people whom he only takes by invitation from existing ones.

Paddi was uncomfortable 'selling' his services, so he wrote what he calls a *Welcome Book* which he sends to customers before they come to the practice. In it he describes what the customers can expect when they arrive at the practice and why long-term dental procedures are important if you want to keep your teeth for the rest of your life. Customers soon arrived wanting to buy the kind of high-quality dentistry Paddi was comfortable providing.

All these little things that Paddi has changed in his business completely transformed his patients' dental experience. They were blown away by the attention to detail. They felt very special and actually liked coming to see him!

Paddi attributes a lot of his success to what he calls these Critical Non-Essentials® or CNe's (pronounced *see nees*) for short. In this area it is clear: Paddi has identified some critical and fundamental drivers of human behaviour. How do customers judge your business? And how would they describe your business to their friends (if at all)?

In this book, and in his own unusual way, Paddi focuses on those differentiating factors — the little things and his attention to detail — that helped to enhance his "brand" in his customers' minds. Although Paddi's insights come from the field of dentistry, I believe these insights are fundamental to all customer service experiences, in any industry.

Interestingly, Paddi does no advertising. His practice is not even listed in the phone book. All Paddi's business comes by word-of-mouth from satisfied customers. He has to be doing something right!

I commend this book to you as one of the more intriguing customer service books I have been fortunate enough to discover.

I hope you find this story as interesting as I have.

Michael Hawker
CEO, Insurance Australia Group

SIMPLE, BUT NOT EASY!

The CNe's are simple ... but they are not all that easy!

1

SIMPLE BUT NOT EASY

The CNe's are simple ... but they are not all that easy!

---

ver the three and a half decades that I have been in commerce my life has become much easier and far happier than it was when I started out. I have noticed that many people actually become less happy as they progress in the business world, so I thank my lucky stars.

My good fortune is due in great part to two important concepts that I have uncovered. The first and most important of these concepts is:

'Business should be designed to give happiness'.

This is the subject of my first book, *Building the Happiness-Centred Business*.

Not far behind in importance to me is the principle of the CNe's:

'The non-essentials in business are of critical importance to your overall success.'

That is the subject of this book.

A Little History

For a long time I laboured under three commonly held misconceptions:

- That my customers understood and judged the core part of my business (the quality of the dentistry) in a similar way that I did.

- That my customers' opinion of my expertise was solely based on their sound judgment of the quality of the goods and services I supplied to them (the dentistry).

- That the non-core areas of my business (the general tidiness, décor etc) were of far less importance to my customers than the core areas (the dentistry).

My ideas have changed over the years:

- Now I realise that customers don't understand much about what I do, and so they judge the quality of my work far differently than I, or any other dentist would.

- Customers base their opinions of quality on many things, the actual dentistry being a small part.

- And I now believe that the 'non-core' areas of my business are very, very important contributors to peoples' perception of what I do.

I call these areas, these non-core parts of business, the Critical Non-Essentials® (CNe's for short). I named them so because many people act as if they don't matter much, but in fact, they seem to be critical to most business success!

My changes in perception came to me gradually, but I can trace their germination to a particular event.

Restaurant Conveniences

Many years ago I was talking to a friend who had visited a local restaurant the previous evening. As people do, she was waxing lyrical about her interesting experience there.

The story she told to me was of a great meal she'd ordered (mango chicken with a peach sorbet to follow), the tasteful décor (a sort of modern, French Empire) the unobtrusive but caring service, and quite reasonable prices.

My friend is a good storyteller and she soon had me convinced that it was to this very eatery that I should go for my next romantic evening.

However, as it turned out, I had made my decision too early – I had yet to hear the climax of her story! I could tell we were coming to the ending of her entertaining tale, however it was not the fabulous positive wrap-up that I had expected.

"Unfortunately!" she continued her story, "Unfortunately, during the meal I had to leave Eric (her husband) to visit the rest rooms. Well, when I eventually found them, I was nearly sick! They were absolutely disgusting!"

Now, I won't offend you with my friend's description of the nature or disgustingness of the conveniences at the back of this establishment. Needless to say, it was graphic.

"Well, I felt that if they let their bathrooms get into that state, imagine what could be happening in the kitchens without us knowing about it. I bet they didn't worry overmuch about their cleanliness, let alone the quality of their meals!

"Well, soon after, Eric and I made our excuses and quickly left the restaurant; I just couldn't face my food again after what I had seen!"

I am sure that my friend spiced up the story a little because most people story-tell with a bit of poetic licence. I assumed that she had made the good bits better than they really were and the bad bits a little more awful than they really had been, because it's what people do when they tell stories. I made some allowance for that. Nevertheless, my desire to eat at this establishment quickly waned.

Sad to say, even knowing that the story was probably a little unfair did not stop me repeating it to a couple of other friends — because, like most people, I like telling juicy stories. And if I embellished my version of the story a little ... well, that's just what everyone does, right?

Perhaps the friends to whom I retold my 'juiced-up' story also retold the story to their friends and perhaps they embellished it a little as well. I don't know that they did, but I wouldn't put it beyond the realms of possibility!

Being in business myself and interested in how customers come to their view about a particular enterprise, I mulled over the story my friend had told me and the subsequent events. A few days later, unable to resist the temptation to find out the truth of the matter, I visited that notorious restaurant ....

Restaurant Conveniences (cont.)

I noted the opulent décor. The food certainly smelt appetising, and the waiters were smartly attired. It looked and felt like a great place to eat. But before I committed myself to order from the extensive menu, I made my way to the bathroom...

The men's room in question was at the back of the building, separate from the main restaurant, not air-conditioned, and it was shared by a couple of other businesses in the same block. With some trepidation and keeping a handkerchief close, I tentatively poked my head around the door.

Interestingly, things were not quite as I had expected. In fact, the men's room was really no worse than many other commercial bathrooms I have been in. The place could have done with a cleaning and there was no soap to wash with, but I have certainly seen (and even used) worse conveniences.

5

I was disappointed. I had expected to feel at least gratified that my Hep-A shots were up to date! Thinking that perhaps this was a misogynist establishment and females had been relegated a more unsanitary backroom, I waited till no one was around and took a tentative peak into the ladies room. Alas, I was disappointed again. The room differed in a few details (as you would expect) but otherwise was much the same and certainly no worse than the corresponding male ablutions.

I returned to the restaurant. I was tempted to be fair and test their food, but my friend's emotional story had struck too deep for that. I made an excuse and left without ordering.

I never did see what caused my story-telling friend's grave concern, however on consideration, I think what had struck my friend was the contrast between the opulent nature of the restaurant and the very ordinary washrooms – rather than their absolute state. Perhaps it seemed incongruous to her that such an establishment could have such basic amenities.

The difference between the standards maintained in the restaurant and that of the rest room made for such a shock to her system that it inspired her to embellish the facts in order to make a juicy story.

It was still some years later that I thought about that incident and others like it. I pondered on the nature of perceptions and realities. I thought deeply about our love of scandalous stories and the tendency for embellishment that story-tellers have. And I considered the tendency we have to judge the quality of the core products of a business (for example, restaurant food) by the quality of the incidentals (for example, the restaurant toilets).

It was some time later still that I learned to understand and harness these foibles of human nature and I coined the name *Critical Non-Essentials*® and the acronym *CNe's*.

Non-Essential

The problem with CNe's is that they are <u>non-essential</u>. By definition, they are things that lie outside the necessary or core part of a business — you don't really have to pay attention to them to get by.

Imagine, for instance, that you have a shop that sells loose tea. You are the only supplier of this commodity — you have a monopoly. You have a successful business. Each day all you have to do is sell tea.

You can supply your tea in unlabeled, low-quality paper bags, and it wouldn't matter. If your shop is dirty and dingy, people will still buy from you ... because they have no choice!

However, most of us are not in the enviable position of being a sole supplier in a sellers market. If we only concentrated on the core of our business and did not bother about any of the niceties — the non-essentials — chances are we will not be very successful.

So everyone has to concentrate some attention on these non-essential, peripheral-to-business areas, if they want to prosper. I am sure that you know that already and I am not thinking that this is a great revelation for you.

But what I am proposing to you is that <u>it is wise to go a little farther into this area than is commonly thought reasonable</u>.

I would like to draw to your attention just how critical the non-essentials are to your current business success and also to how much more success you could enjoy by looking at these particular areas afresh and in a more systematic way.

I believe strongly in the importance of these Non-essentials and I am not alone in this view.

Michael Hawker of IAG (one of Australia's largest and most successful insurance companies) said of the CNe's:

"Although Paddi's insights come from the field of dentistry, I believe they are fundamental to all customer service experiences, in any industry."

And from a little further a field, Sir Clive Woodward, the very successful former England Rugby Union coach who led England to Rugby World Cup Victory in 2003, suggests that his Critical Non-Essentials® were an important factor in his incredible series of wins. Clive's story is an exciting illustration of the CNe's at work in an organisational context, but more on that later. (See Chapter 9: *The CNe Advantage* pg 95.)

Simple Message

My message in this book is actually quite simple:

Take care of the incidentals (the CNe's) if you want to have people respect your core product or service. And do things that give your customers a great story to tell about your business – the Super CNe's

However, I suspect that simply stating my message like this will not give you the sudden blinding revelation that my ideas are earth-shattering in their importance. I know for myself that usually I have to see the same thing written in a number of different ways before something finally clicks in my brain and I really 'get it'!

Another difficulty you might have is that it could be hard to translate ideas from my area of concern (dentistry) into your own type of business. If you read further you will find a fanciful tale among the facts as a different way to help make my ideas more relevant and help you to understand the principles of the CNe's far more quickly than I did.

8

So, come join me on a little adventure while I share with you how I came to understand the importance of the Critical Non-Essentials®.

Are you sitting comfortably? Then I'll begin ...

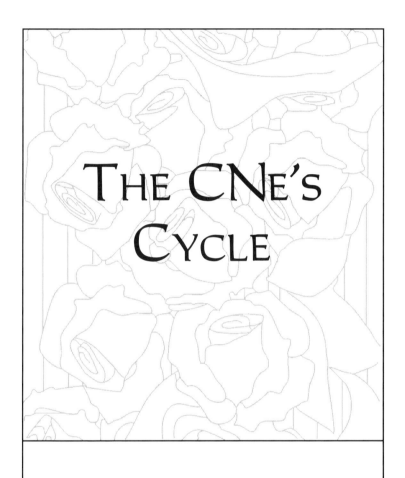

THE CNe's CYCLE

There is an ebb and flow of the tide of business affairs of men and women!

THE CNE'S CYCLE

*There is an ebb and flow of the tide of
business affairs of men and women!*

very now and then I see articles in the
newspaper and magazines about how difficult it
is to create a successful business. The articles
usually quote statistics recently released by some
government department or other that show 75.2% of
businesses (or 81.4% or 68.3% depending on the
economic climate) fail within the first five years.

Usually the author doesn't go much further than saying,
"*Starting a business is risky.*"

In my own neck of the woods I have seen many small
businesses come and go. I'm now getting quite good at
picking those which will meet an early demise.

Usually the people who start the businesses which I think
are doomed to fail spend a lot of time and effort setting up
their company to perform its core function well. However,
they do little to make their business memorable and they
neglect the all-important incidentals that play such a large
part in the success of any enterprise.

Still, a failing business is not a very exciting subject.
Unless, that is, we're talking about a very unusual business
like hippopotamus-sexing or pet-taxidermy.

And maybe when the place in which the businesses exist is
quite extra-ordinary, that also makes the story of their

failing more interesting. With that in mind, perhaps you'll indulge me in a little story of a very unusual business in a very interesting location.

A Business Fairytale

This tale is set in the far off Land of the CNe's, a land that lies at the very edges of my imagination.

In that far-off and fabled land, just as in our own world, there is commerce and industry. And in that land, in strange correspondence with ours, there is also a general lack of awareness of those key (but non-essential) areas of business that we have discussed.

However, in fairytales, as you know, events are usually a bit more dramatic than in real life...

The Land of the CNe's

The Unhappy Land

Once upon a time there was a far off land where the people were poor and unhappy.

If you walked down a lane in any of the villages in that kingdom, you would have seen once-prosperous businesses that had fallen into a state of profound disrepair. Floors were un-swept, shelves empty and shop windows dusty and streaked. Everywhere you went you would have felt an atmosphere of despondency.

The people moved about with an air of hopelessness, and on every street corner strange, unpleasant little beings lounged around indolently, squabbling and noisy. Citizens passing by stumbled over them, cursed and kicked at these creatures until they shambled back into the shadows. These wretched beings that infested the land were called the Ne's – the Non-essentials.

Tradition had it that long ago the kingdom had been cheerful and prosperous, but over many generations trade had slowly decreased and as it did the people sank into poverty and depression. It was also during that time that the Ne's became such a trouble.

The Legend of the Master Inventor

According to legend, the Ne's had been created a long time ago by a Master Inventor to help the people do useful everyday things in their workplaces. At that time they had been a helpful and productive race, very different from the degenerates who were now such a plague on the land.

The Master Inventor had respected the Ne's for their abilities. He didn't call them Ne's, that name came later. He named them the CNe's, the Critical Non-Essentials, because he felt they were vitally important for the prosperity of the businesses in the kingdom, even though they took care of the seemingly non-essential tasks.

The CNe's cleaned and tidied in all the workplaces of the land. They toiled tirelessly, scrubbing, sweeping and polishing so that the shops, mills and factories always shone like new pins.

The land was prosperous and happy. The people were reckoned to be very skilled at their occupations, and customers came from far off countries to buy their wares and to patronise their artisans.

The legend also told of a larger and more magnificent creature, the Super CNe, whose job it was to tell wonderful, stories about the businesses. These stories that the customers repeated to their friends attracted even more customers to the kingdom's enterprises.

Still, I am sure you would not be surprised to hear, that in that far-off land the idea of the nasty Ne's having once being useful and even desirable was difficult for any normal citizen to believe.

The Master Inventor's Mistake

As the legend went, the Master Inventor, though he was very clever, made a fatal error when he told the people that their business success was largely due to his CNe's. The people of the kingdom saw this as a great slur on their abilities. They believed they were successful because they were skilled traders and craftsmen, not because of the menial work done by the little CNe creatures.

Eventually, people grew so tired of the Master Inventor reminding them about his contribution that they persuaded the King to banish him. The King obliged, and the Master Inventor left under a cloud of disgrace, never to return.

The CNe's stayed on, and continued to work as hard as ever, even though the people now regarded them with undisguised scorn. They stopped calling them 'CNe's' as they were obviously critical to no one, and they became derogatorily known as 'Ne's': — the Non-Essentials.

At first, little altered. Business continued as usual and the CNe's went about their work just as they had always done.   Unfortunately things were not to go on in this pleasant way.

After a few months the CNe's started to change!

At first it was just small things: a mark left on a counter, a bit of rubbish remaining in a corner, a streaky window. Then they started to take long naps in the middle of the day, and worked less and less. They no longer kept themselves clean and tidy, and they started to spend time hanging out together on street corners just lazing around. Only a few weeks later, they were doing little useful work at all.

Now the people had to do their own cleaning
and tidying around their workplaces or nothing
was done at all. Mostly, nothing was done, and
the shops, mills and factories began to lose
their sparkling appearance. Gradually they
became untidy, dusty, and dirty.

Where did all the Customers go?

It was not long after the Ne's had ceased work
and the businesses grown more untidy that
business owners noticed the customers were
scarcer.

Previously people had come in droves from the
surrounding kingdoms and principalities. Now,
although the traders' goods and the artisans'
skills had not changed one whit, customers
arrived less often, and when they did come they
seemed far less appreciative than before. They
grumbled more about quality and were far more
likely to complain about prices.

The employees in the kingdom's businesses also
seemed different. They took more sick days,
worked less when they did come to work, and
no longer chatted encouragingly to customers
about the virtues of their masters' and
mistresses' goods.

18

With fewer and fewer happy customers to serve, and less useful work being done, the prosperity in the land gradually decreased.

The people could not understand!
"We are just as skilled as we were before!"
"Our goods are just as fine!"
"It's merely a passing phase."
"A fiscal downturn."
"A micro-economic adjustment."
"A local proto-monetary reflection of a global trend!"

"Things will soon get better again!"

But it wasn't just a *global trend* and it wasn't a *passing phase* either ... and things did not get better! In fact they grew worse and worse until eventually the whole land was caught in the grip of grinding poverty.

What to do?

Something had gone badly wrong in the land of the Ne's. There were no customers, the businesses were unkempt and unprofitable and as for the Ne's, they just lounged around.

What was to be done to make things as they were before, and more importantly, who was to do it?

___

The CNe's Cycle

It's just as easy for a business to lose customers in the real world as it was for the unhappy traders in the Land of the CNe's. Whatever your business, you just have to neglect the "little things" to make customers stay away.

Please let me illustrate my idea of how a customer's mind works. And because we are all customers at some time in our day, and to make it more interesting, let's look at how <u>you</u> might be influenced by business non-essentials.

Imagine that you are driving from one city to another in Queensland, say from Brisbane to Cairns. It's a journey of about two thousand kilometres that takes a couple of days, so at some point, unless you wish to find yourself wrapped around a gum tree, you will have to stop for the night...

Which Motel?

You are a thousand kilometres along your journey, and passing through a coastal town near Townsville that you have never visited before.

It's getting late, the cicadas are chirruping, the air is heavy with humidity and your car's air-conditioner is labouring in the North Queensland heat. Unwilling to face another two hundred kilometres of featureless bitumen to the next town, you decide to rest for the night at one of the motels that line the highway.

There are a dozen or so establishments at which you could stop but you are anxious to find one that will provide a nice cool room with clean sheets and a good shower.

Without stopping, you drive by a Motel that has a flickering neon sign in obvious need of repair. You pass up one with rubbish on the front lawn. You stop at a tidy establishment and gaze into the window of the office only to see unwashed coffee cups and a plate with the remains of a meal left cold and congealed on the counter. You resume your car and drive on.

21

After making a few more rejections, and close to the end of the town you make your stop at a tidy place where the sign is functioning, the front yard tidy and the office is cool and sparkling clean.

Relieved, you book in at this Motel, without examining a room, but confident your expectations will be met.

So, why can I be sure enough of your character to suggest that you did choose in the way I ascribed to you?

From the outside of the motel or at the front desk, you knew nothing of the quality of the bathrooms and beds in any of the motels.

I venture to say that you chose as you did, because you are like 99.8% of customers in the world and know from experience that when the incidentals — signs, gardens, front desk, are taken care of well, the décor and cleanliness of the rooms are likely also to be well maintained.

Occasionally one finds a place where the front office is dirty and where, surprisingly, the rooms are clean and tidy, but most of us learn from hard experience that the rule usually holds.

So it is obvious that the people in the Land of the CNe's had lost a lot of customers because the general tidiness and cleanliness of their villages and business premises suffered from inattention.

The initial chapter in the story of the Land of the CNe's is really a fable with this message:

PADDI POINTER

YOU MAY THINK THAT YOU CAN NEGLECT THE INCIDENTALS, AND THAT AS LONG AS YOUR PRODUCT IS GOOD, THE CUSTOMERS WILL STILL COME. — BUT YOU WOULD BE WRONG!

The ebb and flow of business

In the Land of the CNe's, our little friends degenerated into Ne's, but as you will later discover (because fairytales inevitably have happy endings) the situation was set to improve again: a complete cycle of degeneration and regeneration.

In the real world there is similar cycle that can be observed. It may not be as obvious as in my fairy-tale but it is there if you care to look.

Sad to say, people in business quite forget (or never even know) the simple principle of the CNe's. They can drive a business into the ground very quickly, and someone well versed in CNe principles can just as quickly build it up again.

Here is a story that illustrates this point. (I'm sorry if I betray my pre-occupation with my stomach in taking you to another restaurant, but food has always been very dear to me and I am a great voyeur of businesses that have an alimentary focus.)

Ahmed's Turkish Palace

At his restaurant, The Turkish Palace, Ahmed served large helpings of great food.

There were Turkish pictures on the walls, elaborate brass ornaments and the patrons lounged on an abundance of gaily covered and tasselled cushions. The many ornate ornaments and wall hangings made it feel as though you were seated in a private pavilion in a Sultan's palace.

Middle Eastern music played in the background, incense wafted, and occasionally a belly dancer would gyrate into view. Turkish delights in many flavours were dispensed from overflowing baskets by Ahmed's buxom wife and daughters as they sauntered gracefully among the diners.

23

Genial Ahmed visited tables, waxed lyrical about the delights of Istanbul and gave travel advice to those wishing to see his native land.

After running his restaurant very profitably for a few years Ahmed sold it to John and left for an extended vacation in his beloved homeland.

John was also Turkish but he had anglicised his name. Like Ahmed, John also was an enthusiastic host but he was almost apologetic about his origins and set about subtly westernising the restaurant. The food stayed the same quality, but it gradually developed a more international flavour so that it lost a little of its character.

After a few weeks, John let the belly dancer go. She was an added expense and he justified his action by saying that people came for the food not the entertainment. After all it was a restaurant not a cabaret. Turkish delights were no longer distributed and some of Ahmed's more baroque decoration went to the back storeroom.

The music also changed. John was more partial to popular western music and he felt that his patrons also would not appreciate the wail of the strange Turkish instruments.

Little things began to suffer: the once starched white cloth serviettes were replaced with paper napkins and the laundered tablecloths stayed in the storeroom. Again John felt that these things were an unnecessary expense. After all, he reasoned, it was the quality of the food that mattered to his patrons not the extras.

As it turned out John was wrong. People had come as much for the atmosphere as for the food. They did appreciate the belly dancer and the music – it all made for the experience – and they didn't like eating off bare tables and using paper napkins.

Customer numbers gradually decreased and profits slipped. (John blamed that on economic downturn and the popularity of other ethnic food.) He was forced to compromise on the cleaning of the cushions and carpets and the janitor only came every two days instead of daily as in Ahmed's time.

Pretty soon John was losing money hand-over-fist and was only too happy to sell the restaurant to one of Ahmed's sons, Akbar, for a fraction of what he paid for it.

By the time Ahmed returned from his travels the restaurant was humming again thanks to the attention to detail that Akbar had learned at the side of his father.

Ahmed congratulated his son on a wise purchase and shook his head in wonder that poor old John knew so little about business that he neglected the critically important incidentals.

I wonder if in your part of the world there is the same turnover of restaurant ownership that there is in mine?

I am sure that the CNe-ignorant owners of failing restaurants are just as unhappy and perplexed as the people in the land of the CNe's. And just like their counterparts in that far off land they know that something has to be done. But unfortunately, precisely what that "something" could be is equally unclear to them.

Most businesses that fail have an adequate core product. Their owners have the skill and talents to make useful goods and services and that's a good start. However, how to make a good product is only the first skill they must acquire. At least as important is the knowledge they need to create the systems that impress their customers.

And if you haven't much talent in your chosen area it's just that much more important to know how to impress customers ...

25

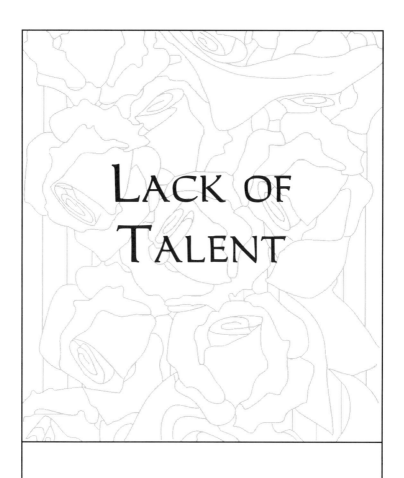

LACK OF TALENT

If you are <u>not</u> good at what you do, you have an opportunity not given to those more gifted.

LACK OF TALENT

If you are <u>not</u> good at what you do, you have an opportunity not given to those more gifted.

---

ack of natural aptitude can be a profound disadvantage in life, but it can also be the catalyst for positive change.

So often those with an innate talent are happy enough with their lives that there is little incentive to push them to invention or change.

It has been said for a long time that necessity is the mother of invention. As a student I had an abounding lack of talent that should have been sufficient to coerce me into all sorts of invention.

And strangely enough, in the Land of the CNe's there was a young inventor in a very similar situation ...

Lack of Talent

Unsuccessful

The ∧Young Inventor

Since all of the problems with the Ne's and the saga of the Master Inventor, the profession of inventing was not at all popular in the Land of the CNe's. However, there were still some who plied that trade and even some who aspired to its ranks.

Near a small village that lay on the banks of a calm river in the Land of the CNe's there was a laboratory tended by an Old Inventor and his apprentice, the Young Inventor.

The Young Inventor lived in the grounds of the Old Inventor's house in a small cottage that also served as his own personal laboratory.

The cottage was of humble design, just a thatched roof and a single room with a tiny curtained window and a door. In the room was a bench, a few battered cupboards to hold tools and a broken trundle bed in the corner. The other corner was occupied by a lop-sided table with a small camp stove and the few old pots and pans in which the Young Inventor cooked his meagre meals.

29

Like all the businesses in the kingdom, the
Young Inventor's workplace was notable mainly
for its untidiness and general decrepitude. Old
plans and pieces of unworkable inventions lay
scattered around. Papers and other debris
covered the floor. Pieces of equipment were
strewn around the benches in such confusion
that it appeared as if a small but powerful
whirlwind had made its way through the room.

The Young Inventor had dreams that one day
he could invent something of earth-shattering
importance, something that would change
everyone's lives for the better and make him
successful.

He laboured hard at his craft but the Old
Inventor was not impressed with his protégé's
skills and often suggested that he should take
up another trade — perhaps grendling, dowsing
or even Dragon-baiting might be more suited to
his talents (or lack of them!).

Lack of Talent

I started my Dental Journey at quite an ordinary university in quite an ordinary town in one of the less populated states in Australia. I was destined, like most of my fellow students, to become quite an ordinary dentist.

And an ordinary dentist, with ordinary skills is essentially what I became — but not for long. In my journey I learned some very interesting things that soon helped me to persuade my customers that I really am, in fact, quite out of the ordinary! And the main reason that I managed to learn these very useful lessons was that I was a very inadequate dental student.

University of Adelaide 1963

For the first two years at University we had studied basic sciences. I was quite reasonable in that area — never outstanding — but certainly adequate enough to be allowed to continue on to the third year.

It was during this third year when we began to perform tasks of a more 'hands on' nature that my deficiencies became apparent. My brain worked soundly enough, but it was not well connected to my two hands.

Things that the other students could do quickly took me far longer. I was invariably the last one sitting at the bench. Assignments like carving teeth from soap or filling holes in plastic model mouths were to me the most difficult tasks I had ever done in my life. It took me hours longer than it should, and my results were less than mediocre.

Eventually my marks became so bad that I was called up to see the Professor.

"What is your problem, Lund?" he began.

"I am not good with my hands," I replied humbly.

He nodded wisely and gave me what I imagine (from not understanding the actual words he used) was the answer to my problem. "Ah, Lund," he diagnosed, nodding sagely, "You are not *manually dextrous!*"

I felt that the Prof. had got to the root of my problem and that things would get better from here on. I left his office feeling far more positive about my future than when I had entered.

Unfortunately, when the meaning of his diagnosis finally became clear, I found it only reinforced my feelings of inadequacy. Yet, over the next few days as I considered my plight, I did see a light at the end of this long academic tunnel.

I began to feel that, rather than just restate my problem in a more esoteric way, the Professor had actually done me a great favour: he had named my malady! And like all maladies, mine benefited from an authoritative label.

Previously I had thought about my difficulty only in a vague way. The name meant I could think about it more objectively, feel less guilty (it wasn't just laziness!) and that I could go to work on my affliction in a positive manner.

In retrospect I am grateful for my lack of innate skill. Talent isn't always as desirable as you might think ... as some wise people have noticed.

Footballer

A talent scout for a first-league team went to visit with the coach of a local football team to find a player that would be suitable to fill a vacancy in the premier side.

You might imagine it was the sort of football played in your part of the world, but in actual fact, because this took place in Australia, it was that brand of football called *Australian Rules Football*. Locally it is known as 'aerial ping-pong' or 'Aussie rules'. (Eight goal-posts, players who take enormous leaps into the air, punch rather than throw the ball and who wear ridiculously short shorts!)

The scout was shown the three best players that the coach had to offer. Any one of them, in the coach's opinion, had definite first league potential. But the scout refused them all!

Undeterred, the scout asked the coach if he could see the other men in the squad and he eventually settled on a player who in the coach's opinion was competent but unimpressive.

When the coach asked him why he had passed over the more talented players for someone who obviously had less skill, the scout replied,

"The players you first showed me were naturally talented and found the game effortless. They wouldn't find it easy to listen to advice about improving their game from someone like me who has little skill on the field. And they would tend to do their own thing because that is what has always worked for them. No matter how hard I might work with them they would improve little."

"On the other hand, the less naturally talented player that I chose has had to work hard, think carefully about his game and heed the advice of others. He will be more open to suggestion and invention and with hard work will eventually become outstanding!"

So do not worry if you find your work is difficult. Those who find work easy will spend little time thinking of better ways to do their tasks. If you are struggling, the chances are you will work out better methods that others wouldn't have thought of and eventually you will become respected for what you do!

Be thankful for any lack of talent and difficulties. It is this deficiency that will allow you to shine in the future and end up ahead of more naturally talented people, just like the tortoise in that mythical race.

PADDI POINTER

Do not be discouraged by lack of talent

Still, it's easy to say that now. At the time my lack of *manual dexterity* was a dark cloud that showed no silver lining.

Further Setback

My education continued relatively uneventfully but nevertheless unsuccessfully. I began to participate in the heady pleasure of University life and for the next year or so late night-study was replaced by late-night revelry.

Finally, inevitably, I had to pay the piper. In late 1966, my lack of talent (aided and abetted by a profound attack of sloth and dissipation) caused me to fail my fourth year of Dentistry!

It seemed the powers-that-be felt that I did not have the basic skills and knowledge to make it in my chosen profession.

Perhaps this was the dark-night before the dawn and the much-needed catalyst for my inventive streak. Or perhaps it was that the path of my life had led me into a deep, dark cave from which there was no escape!

Soon you will know the answer!

34

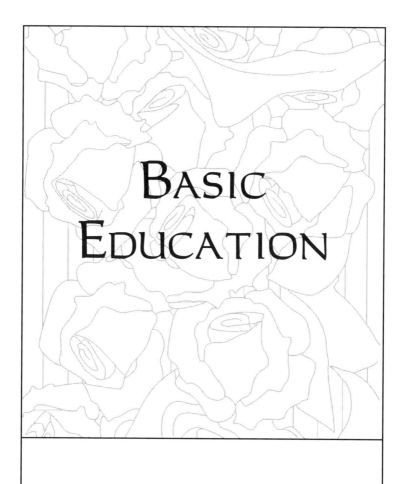

BASIC EDUCATION

Unless you have a sound product, creating
any number of CNe's will achieve little.

BASIC EDUCATION

---

*Unless you have a sound product,
creating any number of CNe's will
achieve little.*

---

rom the title of this book and all my talk about the importance of the 'little things' you may be forgiven for believing that I am advocating that you neglect your core skills and concentrate on the showier parts of your business — far from it!

I firmly believe that the quality of your products and services should be a fundamental goal.

If you try to use CNe's, as you can, to promote the image of a 'quality business' to customers and they later find that there is no quality in what you offer, they will feel very cheated.

Customers are not stupid and can only be fooled for a while by substandard goods and service merely dressed up to impress.

Everyone in business needs to know what they're doing if they want more than short term success. And that takes education!

Basic Education

Prospectus

Eventually the Young Inventor grew tired of his master's criticisms. "Education is the answer to my problems," he deduced. "With more knowledge I will become a better inventor, my master will be happy to recommend me to the Inventor's Registration Board, and I will become a full fledged Professional."

He glanced again at the subjects on the prospectus he had received that morning from the Merlin Inventors College...

Systemic Inventing 103

Practical Prestidigitation 661

Inventology 142

Here was the stuff he needed! Finally, he had found a place where he could learn the skills of inventing.

And so on the first fine day in early spring, he put away his tools, drew the shutters on the laboratory's one window and locked the front door. After taking a final walk through his small garden, he bade good-bye to his master,

37

and set off on a journey of many leagues to commence his training at the finest Inventors' School in the kingdom.

———————————

Basic Education

The Young Inventor had the right idea, basic skills are so very important. However, for me, in my chosen field, just getting the basics right was a rather difficult objective to reach.

University of Adelaide — Late 1965

At the end of my second attempt at passing my fourth year at Dental School an incident occurred that was to change my life.

Learning the 'Stuff'

Having failed my exams the previous year, I had finished my second attempt at the Fourth Year exams. And I had not gone very well in my second try at this test!

In particular I had again failed to satisfy the examiners in regards to my knowledge of *Periodontics* — gum treatment. And so I was required to take a supplementary examination in this subject.

If I failed this hurdle, I would be expelled from the university under the notorious clause 5C of the university regulations. (You have to pass all of the subjects in the year at one go ... and you only get two tries.) That would be the end of my fledgling career.

The exam was to take place towards the end of the summer holidays, and for these holidays, I had a job driving a taxi.

My aim at the time was to work hard at my taxiing and make some money to support my habit (motorbikes). Oh, and I was going to read a *Periodontics* book that I had borrowed from the library. (After supporting a car and a motorbike, I never had enough money left for buying such luxuries as textbooks.)

At the end of the holidays, I planned to return to take the exam, but it did not loom large in my vision of summer sun, money, beaches and bikini clad girls admiring my shining motorbike. I never thought very much about failure or the consequences of failing (expulsion, if you remember). I wasn't thinking very much about the distant future at all in those halcyon summer days.

Luckily for me, one of the heads-of-department at the university called me to his office. He made me listen to a few home truths for which I am eternally grateful.

"Do you realise, Lund," he said, "that if you fail this supplementary exam you are out of here? You'll be on the street selling real estate or repairing motorbikes!" (I had a bad reputation for messing with my motorbikes and was once banned from the clinics for a whole week because of the state of my oil-ingrained hands.)

The good doctor didn't have to say much more. He was being very sincere. Not, I think, because he liked me (which I suspect he didn't – I was not very likeable then) but perhaps because he just thought it sad for someone to flunk out so far into the course. Anyway, no matter what his motivation, I was moved by his discourse.

I decided that I really had to do something about the upcoming test or else I would be out on my ear!

I knew that I didn't have enough knowledge to pass this exam, so I settled down to do a bit of study for a change ... and I passed. (Well, you already knew that because here I am now talking to you as a dentist.)

I don't believe I came back after the holidays as a changed person, but I was a little wiser and a little chastened from my near academic demise. I had learned an important lesson. It was this:

PADDI POINTER

YOU HAVE TO KNOW YOUR STUFF IF YOU WANT TO SUCCEED.

However, knowing what you are doing – being technically competent in the core part of your business – is not, as I later discovered the be-all-and-end-all. There are other things, even more important, if you want to build a successful, profitable enterprise.

University of Adelaide 1966

During my next year at university, we had to spend a lot of time in the clinics. Up until then the major part of my time was working on 'things' – chemistry equipment, rabbits, mechanical manikins – now I was to inflict my rudimentary skill on the general public!

Excellence is a Virtue

Most students found that the hardest part of their clinical dentistry was working on children (also known as 'Pedodontics' in the secret dental language).

It was hard for most students to persuade a child to sit still and be co-operative long enough to get anything done, let alone to do it well enough to get a reasonable mark from the tutors. For me though, it was different.

Because I am really a child at heart, I discovered I could get on very well with the kids who attended for treatment. I found it far easier to entice them to co-operate with me than to do the actual dentistry. Most of the students found it the other way round.

I had a good time with my young victims, laughing, giggling and making little model animals with the bits and pieces of plastic and paper that were left over from the packaging of the dental disposables. My child patients were so busy playing that they didn't seem to notice what I was doing in their mouths.

I was also lucky enough to have one of the few tutors who encouraged untalented dental students rather than disparaged them as was more the norm. I can't think of his real name, but we all called him 'Tiddy'. (It must have been short for something!)

Tiddy was a real gentleman – just a nice person. He enjoyed dentistry and really seemed to like children. Tiddy believed it important that the children were not traumatised by their dental experience. He seemed to

41

admire my handling of our small charges ... and he gave me good marks!

For the first time in my career as a dental student, I found something that I could do reasonably well. Previously I had been a bit of a *klutz*. Now I found that my work (on children at least) was as good as that of everybody else. And I was getting some praise for a change. Wow!

And so I started to gain pleasure in doing things technically well. It was a pleasure I had never been able to enjoy before and I revelled in it.

As luck would have it, I was blessed with another wonderful customer who helped me in my path to excellence.

Gold Foiled

This lady was my patient in the Year 5 clinic. I'm afraid I have forgotten her name but she was an old lady (old in those days was anyone over forty) who was incredibly pain resistant and didn't complain about anything. She just sat there, let me do my work and then told me how well I was doing.

The other blessing I had in that clinic was a tutor who liked 'gold foil' fillings.

Gold foil fillings are made using a technique in which you take tiny pieces of gold and pound them into the tooth cavity under conditions of extreme dryness. It's a very difficult procedure and is no longer used except by a very few technically excellent – some say atavistic – dentists who mostly live on the West Coast of the United States.

The gold has to be very pure and totally uncontaminated with anything such as saliva or oil from the skin on your fingers. If you are not very careful the whole filling just falls apart. It's a most annoying and frustrating technique!

But if you manage to press the gold pieces hard enough and long enough (until your fingers become numb and small blood blisters form on your fingertips) ... and you pray to the correct dental gods in the correct sequence ... and there is an 'r' in the current month ... then, almost magically, the individual pieces weld together to make a seamless mass that looks like a sparkling piece of gold jewellery set in the white of the tooth.

As I mentioned, luckily for me I was blessed with a lady who was extremely tolerant. She hardly salivated at all and she sat stock still while I pounded the foil into her tooth ... and she even thanked me afterwards!

I did gold foil fillings in this lady's mouth from ear to ear ... in all her teeth's little nooks and crannies. She looked immaculate – a dentist's dream! This is the first time in my life that I had done something really well, and I quite enjoyed it! My only worry was that the poor lady had suffered a lot of trauma at my hands and one of her teeth seemed to be dying as a result of the pounding.

I'm not sure that it was sensible dentistry for this lady. I think other methods of therapy may have been better.

My treatment of her took an enormous amount of time, money and effort. Some of the smaller holes became very large from my ministrations, and some of her teeth did die from all my pounding. But the fillings looked magnificent when finished, and my tutor (you'll remember he was a gold foil fanatic) told me (with a tear in his eye) that they were truly wonderful!

I was given a great mark for my work, eventually graduated, and with my new found skill in the basics of dentistry I imagined that now I was ready to make my mark on the world.

The problem I faced was that the world is not a University and customers have different values from one's teachers and one's peers. In my subsequent thirty years as a dentist I never again did a gold foil restoration!

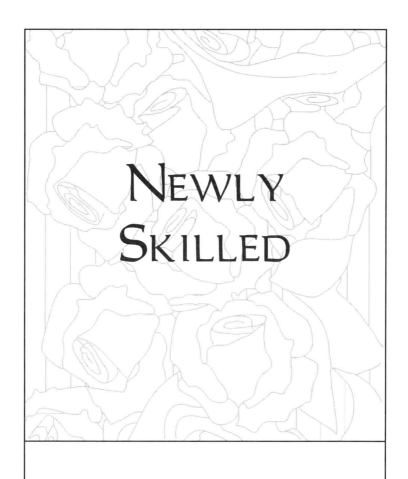

NEWLY SKILLED

Just because you are skilled, it does not mean that customers will beat a path to your door.

Newly Skilled

Just because you are skilled, it does not mean that customers will beat a path to your door.

suppose it's normal that when you finish your education you have a tendency to believe that you now know everything that is worth knowing about your particular vocation.

The young are most knowledgeable when they are young.

It's only after a bit more education and experience that you start to realise how little you know about business generally even though you might have a lot of knowledge about your trade or profession.

Newly Skilled

Home Again

After his long years of study, the Young Inventor, returned to his small, decrepit laboratory in the land of the CNe's. The Old Inventor had retired and kindly allowed the Young Inventor to take up a lease on that meagre building.

After tacking his degree to the wall the young inventor sat down to wait for the customers who would surely be drawn by his newly won qualifications and talent.

"My fortune will now be made," he said. "I have done my study. Now is the time to reap the rewards."

But unfortunately, events did not unfold in quite the rosy way he had envisaged.

A few customers did come to consult the Inventor. They managed to wade through the mess and dirt on his person and in his laboratory to give him small commissions. And a few of these customers sent their friends ... but not very many of them.

What did it all mean? He knew he was good at his job and yet his customers didn't seem to understand ... or care.

"Customers are just stupid," he thought to himself. "They don't appreciate talent when they see it."

And for many months he railed against the unfairness of business and puzzled over how he could improve his lot.

———————

Newly Skilled

When you first start out in business, the fact that you are now able to do something that you have dreamed of for a long time — that you have skills and products that people want to pay good money for — can be a little awe inspiring.

I remember when I first studied hypnosis. Many of the books I read warned of the "Jesus complex": a belief that because you can influence the thinking of others you can perform other miracles as well.

I didn't think much about this problem at the time and I never really felt messianic, but when I first started work as a dentist I did come close to feeling omniscient. I didn't think I knew everything, but certainly 90% of everything.

Oh, the folly of youth!

My first years of dentistry were hard, and they were made far harder still because there were important lessons that I still had to learn.

I had my basic skills. I was good at dentistry — or at least adequate now. However, it was hard for me to make a buck. (Or a pound, as it was in Australia before decimalisation.) Customers did not beat a path to my door and it was difficult to persuade them to buy my wares when they did arrive.

I remember one such client, a forty-ish, affluent man who could easily afford any sort of dentistry ... and he really needed some help!

Treatment Plan

I worked hard at making my examination of this gentleman as comprehensive as possible.

49

I took X-rays, probed for gum disease pockets and charted the results. I made plaster models of his teeth and polished and soaped them so that they looked smooth and sleek.

Just as I had been taught in University, I carefully mounted the models on a mechanical articulator to imitate the movement of his jaws in opening and closing and chewing. And I had written out a most comprehensive treatment plan with a number of options, all carefully documented and replete with photographs.

The time came for me to meet with my patient and present my plan. We sat down together and I told him of the comprehensive reconstruction of his mouth that I envisaged, and I explained all the benefits ... and told him the price: three thousand dollars!

A look of shock and profound distrust hardened his features. "Three thousand dollars", he spluttered. That's a lot of money just to fix teeth when I'm not even sure how long they will last. I shall have to think about that!"

He bade me a polite but cold goodbye, never again to set foot in my practice.

What a waste of my time and effort!

Lack of Trust

All too regularly, when I presented someone with a plan for treatment, I would be rewarded with this same look of distrust. And I remembered what my gentleman patient said about 'lasting' which was polite code for "And I don't even know if you will perform your treatment well!"

As this same scenario was played time and time again with different characters over the next few years, I became sullen and resentful. What was the point of spending a lot of time and effort if people were not going to listen to me and they didn't believe what I said!

The difficulty was that they didn't trust that I was good enough to solve their problem.

I am sure that the trouble I took with my plans and models created a good impression, but my customers saw this as something to be expected from any dentist. They had little experience with dental treatment plans and assumed everyone presented them with the sort of detail that I had done for them.

Now a fellow dentist, on the other hand, would have seen the excellence of my work and been far more impressed than these lay people. Unfortunately I didn't have any clients who were dentists! And without this professional level of judgment, all my planning work was in vain. With my ordinary customers, I just did not generate the level of trust in my professional ability that would persuade them to have my treatment.

It seemed to me that this lack of trust in my skills made for a very inefficient way of doing business. Lots of my time was spent trying to persuade people to buy from me and quite regularly all of my good work would go for nothing.

I needed to find a way to make an impact on my customers that differed from the ways that I would use to impress my peers. I needed someone or something that would whisper in my new customer's ears reassuring words like, "He can do the job well. You can trust him."

But just who (or what) would do that quite escaped me!

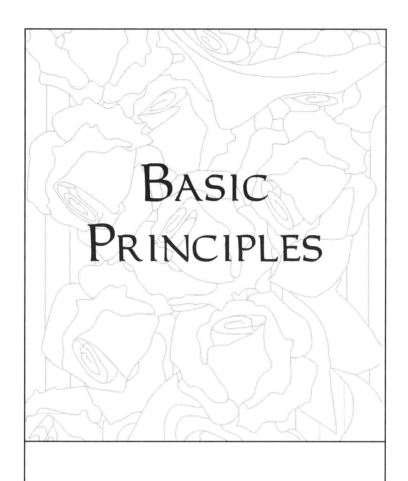

BASIC PRINCIPLES

Appearances are important!
Don't expect the world to judge you fairly.

BASIC PRINCIPLES

*Appearances are important! Don't
expect the world to judge you fairly.*

I have always had the tendency to be idealistic and to believe that circumstances should be a certain perfect way. Often the ways of the world are not what I would wish them to be and the injustice of that upset me.

People should be benevolent and fair and loving. A cat shouldn't get pleasure from torturing its prey before killing it. There shouldn't be horrendous accidents, tidal waves and volcanoes!

However that's just the way it is. Wishing it were otherwise puts me in a position of suggesting that if I had made the world I would have done it differently. And that's a very difficult position to feel comfortable with ... and requires one to fill very big boots!

So gradually I have come to accept things as they are. That is not to say I don't try to change my little corner of the world, but I no longer complain about the laws of physics or try to alter basic human nature.

Over time I have come to work within the parameters the world gives me and to find ways to make my life easier in spite of those parts of it that rankle and annoy me.

I may feel that appearances shouldn't matter, but they do, even to me. I may feel that sometimes my skill is judged unfairly but people are not always fair in their judgements — even me!

Until I could come to those realisations and embrace them, I was not able to understand the principles upon which the CNe's depend. But once my mind was able to accept these realities of life I was ready to turn matters to my advantage ...

Basic Principles

Discovery!

One day in an old box left to him by his grandfather, the Inventor (who was not so young anymore) came across the blueprints for a strange mechanical device. According to the notes on these plans, this was the design for the very machine that the Master Inventor had used to create the original CNe's.

"Perhaps," thought the Inventor, "I could make CNe's for myself.   If there is any truth at all in the 'Legend of the CNe's', having a troop of those little fellows running around would certainly improve my business! What an impression they would make on my customers. Maybe I could manufacture them for the whole kingdom. Wouldn't that be a feather in my cap!"

The Inventor set to work with gusto, following the strange writing and symbols on the old blueprints as best as he was able. For many long winter months he could be heard banging and tapping away in his little laboratory.

But it was slow work, and often he was forced to labour far into the night deciphering the archaic manuscript. Looking for any way to shortcut his task, he brought a few Ne's to his laboratory to question them and see if he could gain any clues to the method of creation of their worthy progenitors, the CNe's.

Unfortunately, the Ne's proved as uncooperative as always and were no help at all. They annoyed him by sitting idly around, getting in the way and making the little laboratory even messier than it had been before. They wouldn't leave when asked and they ate up all his food!

Nevertheless, very gradually, as the Inventor unravelled the Secrets of CNe reproduction from the old documents, a strange machine began to take shape in the centre of his laboratory floor.

Basic Principles

Like the Inventor I had to work hard in pursuit of my goal. But in the real world, to uncover the basic principles of the CNe's and the information that you need to construct them, is less straight forward than it was even for the Inventor.

Unlike the Inventor, I found no ancient plans for a machine to help me to reach my goal. My answer lay in a number of challenging experiences and lessons to help me to understand the old wisdom that made up the foundation upon which the CNe's operate.

Powerful Impressions

My first big lesson was about the power of appearance and how it can change our impression of people. This instruction came during my fourth year at the University of Adelaide.

Housing Problem

Because I spent all of my money on my motorbike, I had little left over for rent and I existed hand-to-mouth in a succession of dingy flats.

My store-cupboard held little but a large sack of rice and tins of cheap sardines. These two staples I combined to make a variety of dishes. Unfortunately, these dishes contained only rice and sardines, and eventually I became vitamin deficient. I had a number of strange afflictions and skin lesions.

In an effort to conserve cash a couple of student friends and I got together to share an old house. This left me a little more money for luxuries like other kinds of foods.

It was not a very salubrious establishment. We had motorcycle parts on the kitchen table and over the floors. We had strung wires across the hall to join the alarm clock to the front doorbell in order to wake us after a night of fermented debauchery. The furniture was rudimentary and threadbare. Small creatures, mould and pathogenic micro-organisms thrived and bred in our kitchen!

The few female visitors that we did receive left quickly, sniffing in disgust. We laughed at this, not fully realising the implications for our social lives.

Eventually, even I found that I could no longer tolerate the squalor, so I found myself a part-time job and moved into a place of my own. I kept it cleaner than the share house, but it was still not a place that I would wish to visit with my present heightened sensibilities.

I started to have a few guests of the opposite sex, and it became my habit to make a very rapid clean-up whenever I felt there was a chance of a visit. But after a while I realised this was not enough.

Young ladies seemed to be able to tell the difference between a quick 'lick-and-polish' and a continuous program of regular household care ... and the difference appeared to matter to them.

They did not seem to like drinking out of the grimy cracked glasses that my male friends and I thought were quite adequate. I began to realise that most girls valued cleanliness and orderliness far more than I did.

Not only did they expect these things (cleanliness and orderliness in household management) but they also used them as a yardstick to measure young men's personal cleanliness — and thus one's suitability to be allowed to be close to their desirable person.

I decided the only way to ensure that my flat was always ready for visitors was to keep it tidy and to have a system for consistently doing just that.

From that time on, I had more successful relationships with young women ... and strangely enough I also began to enjoy having a clean and orderly environment in which to live my (now more exciting) social life. And it was certainly less stressful to keep things neat than to have frantic middle-of-the-night cleaning sessions.

☞ PEOPLE MAKE VALUE JUDGEMENTS ABOUT THE CHARACTER AND TALENTS OF OTHERS FROM THE ENVIRONMENT IN WHICH THEY LIVE OR WORK.

With my newly acquired habits of tidiness and cleanliness in my dwelling, I found that even though my own habits left a lot to be desired, I was making more judgments about others on the basis of their personal hygiene.

Oral Hygiene

She was gorgeous with flowing red hair, beautiful green eyes and long legs, this Art student whom I had chanced to meet in the library.

Unfortunately, Miss Redhead was romantically associated with a good friend of mine, and that made it very difficult when she asked me if I would give her a lift back to her college in North Adelaide!

I acquiesced with some trepidation not wanting to compromise a friendship. As we drove along King William Road and she snuggled closer to me, I began to think that Miss Redhead was interested in more than a just a lift home. The call of my hormones was quite rapidly beginning to overcome my scruples.

From previous visits to this college, I knew that the matron there was not averse to berating young men who returned her charges at a late hour, so I stopped the car at a dark corner, a little way away.

Miss Redhead leaned closer and, inevitably, our lips met. We kissed long, and then again. My arm slid around her soft form of its own volition; she wiggled closer as if in invitation.

The windscreen of the car was becoming comfortably steamed and hiding us from passers-by. A passing headlight softly pierced the misted glass and discovered the highlights in her beautiful red hair. Her green eyes sparkled and my resolve not to do the dirty on my friend was waning.

Unfortunately, the same light also revealed that her single-tooth front denture had loosened a little, and there was a nasty green piece of food caught between it and her natural teeth!

Despite my hormones, my ardour rapidly cooled.

I regained my composure, clumsily made some excuse about an exam, dropped her off and sped away. She was not at all happy and hated me for a long time afterwards. I don't blame her, and I never told her why.

Even though I realised her dental hygiene had little to do with this young lady's worth as a person, nevertheless, I was still influenced by the flaw in her appearance ... just as I was influenced by the positive: her lovely hair, legs and eyes.

I wonder how many budding romances have been spoiled by a small slip of grooming!

FOR GOOD OR FOR BAD, WE DO USE THE PERSONAL APPEARANCE OF OTHERS TO MAKE JUDGEMENTS ABOUT THEIR CHARACTER AND VALUE.

A couple of years after the incident with Miss Redhead, following my graduation, I moved to England to study to be an Oral Surgeon. I managed to get a training post that gave me lots of experience.

I had almost forgotten the affair with the red-haired young lady. I understood that I was affected by the look of others — especially young females — but I did not consider that my personal appearance might also affect those self-same people. I believed that my appearance should not matter. I felt that people should judge me on who I was and what I knew.

It was not too long afterwards that I wished I had understood the importance of the 'Oral Hygiene' incident and its implications about how people regarded me. Perhaps I was paying for my sins against the poor red-headed girl.

Fellow of the Royal College – FRCDS

To become an Oral Surgeon in Australia in those far off days, one had to do a succession of hospital jobs and pass exams to be a Fellow of the Royal College of Surgeons in London.

The exam consisted of two parts: the Primary Examination which was mostly about basic medical sciences, and the Secondary Examination which was about diseases and their treatment.

The Primary was reckoned to be very hard, and often took a number of attempts, while the Second part was thought to be a lot easier.

Well, I passed the Primary Examination at my first attempt, but I had four tries at the Second Examination. Each time I passed everything but one subject and each time it was a different subject. I remember feeling very perplexed about this whole situation.

A typical attempt at the exam went like this:

I would prepare thoroughly for this test then drive down to London on the day of the exam. I would arrive a little dishevelled in my regular clothes and would laugh to myself at the other candidates with their strange striped suits and briefcases. They looked 'Oh so professional' and 'Saville Row'.

Chatting with them, I was always happy with the depth of my knowledge, and I felt I had a better chance than they of passing the examination.

In retrospect I now know that wasn't true. I did have a lot of technical knowledge, but I didn't look the part. With my long hair and colourful shirt, I appeared as though I would be more at home in a hippie commune than in a long established and very conservative surgical college.

My appearance had been unimportant for the mostly written and relatively anonymous Primary Exam. Unfortunately, the Second Examination was mainly oral, and these *viva voce* were taken by surgeons who were members of the College. And as you can imagine they wanted someone who would fit in and looked as though he would be a worthy collegian – a credit to the establishment. This was definitely not me!

I am sure they believed that someone who dressed as I did, who obviously did not realise that clothing was important, would not be a credit to the good name of the College. And so they did not let me in!

It was not until a few years later when I came home to Australia where things are more relaxed – and I had learned to dress more appropriately – that I finally managed to pass the second part of the examination.

Even after my experience with the power of personal appearance and the FRCDS, I still had that same lesson repeated before I really understood it – talk about dumb!

Take the case of teeth and their appearance:

Brasher Gnashers

As we get older our teeth darken, and so older people should have darker teeth in their dentures so that they appear 'natural'. So I followed the wisdom that I had learned in Dental School that patients should be given the colour of false teeth that fitted in with their appearance and was appropriate to their age.

Unfortunately, the usual reaction to my 'natural' look was something like this: "I showed my new teeth to my friends and they thought they weren't white. Why aren't these teeth whiter? I have spent all this money and you've made them all yellow!" (I think there was the unspoken thought that this was somehow a cost cutting exercise and they were being cheated. The darker teeth I had supplied them must have been cheap Chinese copies of the proper white ones that were made in Australia!)

I would explain, "This colour I chose is the one that nature would have chosen for someone of your age. I have carefully matched the shade of the teeth to your hair and skin colouring. Lighter teeth would look artificial ..." But it was to no avail!

Often as not I was forced to remake the dentures with a lighter colour of teeth.

Logic pales into insignificance beside the need for approval!

Later I was to learn a lesson about the appearance of teeth in an even more personal way.

My *Teeth*

I have not been blessed with particularly good teeth, and they need constant attention. Just like the cobbler with his shoes, I tend to put off vital dental work. I've had many chipped back teeth, yet I waited ... and waited ... and waited for an appropriate time to have them treated. That time never seemed to come.

But when I chipped a front tooth, it wasn't long at all before I had my first negative comment. My nurses had a quiet word with me. Couldn't I see that it would affect business? Customers would think I wasn't a good dentist because I didn't look after my own teeth!

When I realised I was subject to the same rules that I applied to everyone else, I was into my friend's dental chair before you could say 'local anaesthetic'!

Eventually, the effect of this incident added to those that came before it and began to have a definite influence on the way I thought. And so — but unfortunately far later in my life than it is for most people — I finally came to the realisation that personal appearance is important!

And in just the same way as my explorations of courtesy (that led to my first book *Building the Happiness-Centred*

Business) allowed me to see politeness as a wonderful tool for communication, I began to perceive appearance as a useful tool to improve others judgement of me. I decided to work within a system that really seemed, to me, to be basically unfair.

I now know that how things 'look' is very important, but even so, I do not believe that judgement by appearance is always useful or 'good' – it's just the way the world is.

Sometimes social customs are extreme and people are forced into all sorts of strange behaviours to conform to societal norms. Indigenous to some cultures you'll find six-inch heels on shoes, large facial tattoos, pierced lower lips, and necks stretched by numerous metal bands – things which, in themselves, cannot be particularly beneficial to the owners.

They are, however, what a particular society has come to believe is an important part of a 'good appearance'. And society's judgement is definitely not always fair and reasonable to those under sharp scrutiny.

Unfair world

I remember a time when I was toiling in London under the socialised National Health System. I was quite a good National Health Dentist compared with many, but still my standards fell quite alarmingly from the levels I had felt were reasonable in Australia. I was working in a surgery in New Cross – a working class area – grim and grimy.

I was rushing one day, and my next patient was a gentleman who required what was called 'scaling and polishing'. This was a very primitive procedure that involved scraping the scale (or plaque) off a person's teeth. In those days under the NHS, you would quickly whip around with a pumice-coated brush to give things a bit of a polish. On average the whole process would take about ten minutes. If you took more than ten minutes, you didn't make money ... and you didn't eat!

Guilty Rewards

On this particular day I had only about five minutes in which to see my next patient. I'll call him 'Patient A'. He turned out to be a big, burly, battleship of a man. Patient A had enormous teeth that were covered in hard, thick scaly stuff. Here was my worst dental nightmare. Five minutes to clean those monsters. I would have needed a whole day and a jackhammer!

Now, I'm not a big man, and I had only a little hand scraper, so in five minutes I didn't make much of an impression on his scale. But still, lying through my teeth, I told Patient A that I was finished, thanked him for his time and sent him out to reception to sign the government payment forms.

I felt quite guilty that I hadn't done a very good service but, mind you, I was not conscience stricken enough to call him back and do it better. However, I promised myself that, when this gentleman returned in six months, I would make sure that I set aside plenty of time to do the job properly.

Soon my thoughts left Patient A, and I was off again on the National Health treadmill — cutting holes and packing amalgam so fast that it splattered the walls!

Half an hour later Betty, the lady receptionist, came back to see me and told me that Patient A was very impressed with my scaling.

Huh?

"He said you were very, very gentle and he wanted me to thank you. The other dentist that treated him six months ago took half an hour to do the same job you had done in five minutes ... and had made his gums bleed!"

I retired to my room, puzzling the ways of the world...

In truth, the other dentist who was so castigated by Patient A had in all probability done the scaling far more thoroughly than I had. Of course, he had made Patient A's gums bleed. They would have bled with any decent dentist. The scale was right down underneath his very inflamed gums. They would have bled for me too if I had done anything more than my very cursory job.

So, I was constrained by time and didn't have enough of a conscience to do the job properly and yet I was rewarded for it! Slapdash me – I got the praise! The poor dentist who had done the scaling thoroughly was denigrated. Where was the justice in that!

PADDI POINTER DO NOT EXPECT YOUR CUSTOMERS TO VALUE THE SAME THINGS THAT YOU AND YOUR PEERS VALUE.

Important Delivery

At New Cross I had learned that clients' judgments are not always objective and valid. However, sometimes they are!

Ice-Cream

Let's say that I am an ice-cream vendor and I'm selling home-made ice cream.

You buy a choc-ice from me and notice that my hands are dirty and my ice-cream scoop is rusty.

Even if I boast to you that my ice-cream is 27% creamier and has twice the flavour of the opposition, I'll bet you wish you had bought from my competitor instead. And you'd probably ditch my ice-cream at the first opportunity, wouldn't you?

Throwing away the ice-cream I sold you may well be a wise decision on your part. If my hands and implements don't look clean, it may mean that they are really are not clean and that I was less that scrupulous with hygiene when I made the ice-cream. And if I am careless with my hygiene, it may well mean that, in spite of the great flavour, my ingredients are not fresh and good for your health.

There is often a very logical basis for judging a product on the quality of its delivery. As a paradigm it serves us well. But customers are not always in possession of the facts. As we saw with Patient A, sometimes customers judgements are not wise. However, the following rule holds true whether or not you feel customers are being reasonable:

THE WAY YOU APPEAR TO DO SOMETHING IS OFTEN MORE IMPORTANT THAN WHAT YOU DO!

So, now I knew that the world does not always judge fairly and I had learned that appearances really are important. With this knowledge I had discovered the basic principles on which the CNe's operate. Now my task was to do something useful with the knowledge I had gained ...

FIRSTBORN

The first creation is the most difficult.

FIRSTBORN

The first creation is the most difficult.

---

aving your first child is always the hardest. (So I am told by those who should know.) Everything is so strange that first time — there is so much uncharted territory!

Once you know the basic principles of parturition you might assume that the whole birth process would be simple. But it's not so with first human birth and it certainly is not so for first-time CNe inventors.

The forthcoming description only takes a few thousand words, but in reality it took both the Inventor and me many months of hard work, and false starts...

Firstborn

Parturition

The Inventor *laboured* on and on in his laboratory and, in spite of the difficulty of the task and the distraction of the Ne's, one fine autumn day the 'CNe Generator (for that is what he called the strange machine) was finally completed.

And that very evening the Inventor decided to try out his creation.

Standing resolutely in front of his CNe Generator, the Inventor pulled down the largest of the switches on the control panel, selected a book-sized punched card that he had laboriously copied from the Master Inventor's diagram and pushed it firmly into a slot in the machine's main panel.

Strange mechanical noises increased rapidly and the machine's dials and lights flickered in synchronisation with its frenetic activity, then it quietened for a few minutes as it seemed to digest the information on the card.

One after the other, he placed three more punched cards into the machine's slot and the same series of events occurred.

A few minutes after he had fed in the fourth card, the device vibrated and hummed even more loudly and agitatedly than before. The lights of the room dimmed with the drain of enormous power, and an eye-searing flash lit up the interior of the machine.

Just when it seems as if the device would be split by the energy it contained, it suddenly stilled. The machine fell silent as if exhausted from its pyrotechnics.

"Click, clack."

Without warning, the conveyor belt at the front of the machine suddenly began to rotate, breaking the silence with its clockwork sound.

There was a movement in the central chamber of the machine. The curtains obscuring the entrance were set swaying and a few seconds later, a strange figure emerged. Squinting slightly, a fully fledged CNe was delivered by the conveyor into the lights of the laboratory.

The small being blinked, drew itself up to its full, diminutive height, and stepped carefully to the floor. The Inventor threw down his clipboard, hugged the little creature nearly to death and together they danced jubilantly around the machine.

As soon as the Inventor, unused to such exertion, stopped to catch his breath, the newborn creature picked up a broom and purposefully set to sweeping up the mess around the machine, like the good little CNe it was.

The Inventor had done it! He'd created a CNe!

Now things were set to change around this little laboratory!

Firstborn

Mount Gravatt 1975

After I returned to Australia, I wandered around for a year or so working here and there until finally buying my own dental practice. As I remember I paid just $800 for it (a very small amount even in those far-off days). The business had been owned by a gentleman who was actually a Dental Technician, licensed under an archaic Government Act of the 1920's — it was a strangely old-fashioned place Queensland in the 70's.

First Business

No sooner was the ink dry on the paperwork than an alarming thought struck me: *Now I am the boss!* It was a scary idea!

No one is standing over me with orders and advice. The responsibility is all mine. I will sink or swim on my own merit. It was a heavy and unfamiliar burden. Every responsibility to make my new venture succeed rested on my shoulders!

Well, the strategy that had rewarded me most in University and subsequent study had been to do the technical part of my job really, really well! I had not always excelled because I wasn't naturally good with my hands, but when I did, I had been praised. Surely what would please my discerning tutors would please my far less knowledgeable customers!

And so I decided that the way to make my fortune in Dentistry was to do every part of it with absolute excellence. I put my whole effort into being the best technical dentist I could possibly be!

I did wonderful restorations of people's teeth. I discovered the 'rubber dam' — a famous dental perversion, greatly respected by dentists as a way of performing highly detailed treatment. It is very difficult stuff to use and can be quite unpleasant for patients.

I did everything with rubber dam, even though it nearly killed me — and my patients!

I tried very hard to be precise, paid attention to detail, always used the very best materials, and I constantly read journals to discover the most up-to-date techniques.

All of this hard work did earn me some kudos from my fellow dentists, but not a lot from my clients!

My customers seemed to respect the work I did because it lasted well. And they did admire the fact that I worked hard and sweated a lot while fixing their teeth. They noticed I was proud of what I did, and I think that counted for something — but not very much.

However, customers seemed far more concerned with their bill than my skill and so, only very slowly and with great effort did I build up my practice.

As I look back now, I can imagine what my patients were saying about me:

"He's a really slow dentist. It takes ages and you do have to sit still or he gets annoyed ... a bit stressed-out and edgy ... and expensive."

All in all, my customers didn't seem to like me terribly much. They were not really interested in sending their friends to see me, and I found it very hard to persuade anyone to have anything other than the absolute bare minimum of dentistry.

A Paradox of Business

I had always imagined that people in business were rewarded in proportion to their craftsmanship or the quality of their goods. Now I started to realise that this was not always so.

I knew of people who worked very hard and were good at what they did, but they didn't seem to be very successful. Yet there were others who appeared to have little talent (or to have a very average product) who ended up carrying their money to the bank in a wheelbarrow.

This just didn't seem fair, and it was a great puzzle to me. Some people who had no obvious talent in their trade succeeded while others who had far less aptitude became wildly successful. Why was it that some people did well when others, who seemed at least as skilled and deserving, starved?

Learning from George (George I)

> At one time I had a receptionist named George. George was cultured, kind ... and gay as a badger! (My mother says this expression was originally, 'Gray as a badger,' but I like my saying better!)
>
> George was a natural receptionist: a good conversationalist, hard working, personable and he charmed the pants off the ladies (figuratively speaking). George would ask people about their day, sympathise with them in their problems, congratulate them in their successes and join them in a cup of tea that he always seemed to be making for them. Customers liked George.
>
> As I mentioned before, I was now a good technical dentist — I knew what I was talking about. However, not many patients decided to have all the treatment that I thought best for them. Most listened politely and then did nothing about their problems. It was frustrating and not very profitable.
>
> But on the rare occasions when George told them it was in their best interest to have a particular sort of

treatment, they would listen! How strange! I was the technical expert. I knew what I was talking about. Why did they listen to George rather than to me? I was puzzled ... and a little annoyed.

Here I was out the back in the 'salt mines' doing the dentistry, and there was George in reception, drinking tea, chatting and enjoying himself! (George worked hard, too, but that's difficult to remember when you hear laughter from the other side of the door while you're sweating away, elbow deep in some poor unfortunate's mouth.)

People treated George as a friend and confidant. And me? Well, I was treated as some sort of cruel torturer and they spoke very little to me. I thought it was all a bit unfair, but there didn't seem to be much I could do about it.

What is important, really?

If there were ever a choice between technical perfection and my patients comfort or happiness I would always decide on perfection.

Now this is all well and good if it is to the patient's benefit, but often this was not the case.

I would spend hours carving my fillings so that they were perfect representations of natural teeth. It didn't matter to me that the exact shape was not functionally important and did not lead to increased longevity of the filling. I did it for myself, because it made me feel good!

I didn't believe that the niceties and courtesies of business were important, and so I neglected them. I didn't understand the power of what George did. I felt that the dental technical things were what would give me success so I pursued them to the detriment of the comfort and happiness of my customers.

Technical excellence certainly is important, but as I later learned, not as important to people as a kind word and a bit of thoughtful hospitality. George's conversations and cups of tea were far more important to my clients than all my perfect amalgam, gold foil or rubber dam.

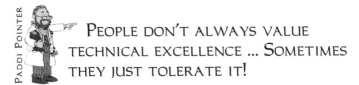

PEOPLE DON'T ALWAYS VALUE TECHNICAL EXCELLENCE ... SOMETIMES THEY JUST TOLERATE IT!

I needed to make major changes in my business.

It is obvious now, but it was not at all clear to me then. For there was one more lesson that I had to learn from George before a glimmer of understanding lighted in my brain.

Learning from George (George II)

George was always cleaning and tidying. At the time I felt he was a little too fussy. George would clean anything that stayed still for more than a few seconds. He was obsessive (or so I thought).

George believed that because we were running a dental business, everything should be really clean — not only the surgery areas but the reception room as well. I was not convinced that it was worth all the effort!

However, all that began to change when I overheard two lady patients who felt differently.

Lady1 to Lady2, "Oh, it's so nice to be in such a clean place."

Lady2 replied, "The last dentist I went to had old cigarette butts in the waiting-room ash trays, and when I lay in his chair I could see little cobwebs on the air-conditioning outlet. All the time I was lying there I couldn't help wondering about the instruments he was putting in my mouth!"

Hmm... thought I, *Perhaps George is on to something!*

Eventually I came to a greater understanding of the power of the 'little things' to influence people's opinion. It was a very gradual process for me, but eventually, a few years after George had left my employ to return to England I could understand enough to recognise three points:

1. You may believe that it is the core of your business that people judge you by. And so it is ... to a certain extent, but most customers do not really understand much about your core expertise or which factors they should use to judge its quality.

2. Other experts in the same line of business can easily make logical judgements. They know what to look for. They know what's important. A cobbler knows how to rate the quality of shoes, a banker knows how to judge banking, and an accountant can recognise accounting expertise. But customers are usually not experts in the business they're patronising, and they don't know what the signs are that indicate if you are highly skilled, mediocre or useless in your field.

3. In the absence of a deep knowledge of your product or service, customers will use their opinion of your performance of 'household' tasks as a basis for their judgment of your product quality.

And I could state with certainty the following:

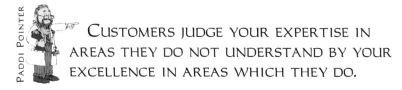

PADDI POINTER

CUSTOMERS JUDGE YOUR EXPERTISE IN AREAS THEY DO NOT UNDERSTAND BY YOUR EXCELLENCE IN AREAS WHICH THEY DO.

My first CNe

Armed with my new insight into the power of the 'little things', I decided to set to work to make a few changes. The area I decided to tackle first was our 'pre-patient set-up'.

Up to this point we had never really managed to do everything we thought was needed to prepare for a customer's arrival. When we talked about the subject everyone seemed to know what had to be done, but there never seemed to be enough time to do it all. And even when there was time, tasks were forgotten or not completed correctly.

So I met together with my Nurses, and we created a list of all the tasks that were needed to prepare for the day and described in detail any which were complex. In effect we were making our first CNe — a system for doing the little things of business.

At the top of the sheet there were titles and beneath were a series of description lines like this:[*]

Task	Mon	Tue	Wed	Thur	Fri
Put out flowers	*P*	*M*	*P*	*N*	*M*
Nibbles	*M*	*A*	*A*	*P*	*M*

The task descriptors were shorthand for a series of tasks like:

FLOWERS: Put out the flowers, change the water, cut the stalks, add the sugar and bleach to the flower water.

NIBBLES: Clean plate, doily, fresh fruit, dried fruit, 'eat me' sign.

COFFEE TABLE: Dust, place the hand cream, hand bell and customer information book.

---

[*] If you'd like to see an exact copy of the entire *Daily Tasks Checklist* that Paddi uses to run his business, please visit www.PaddiLund.com and look for *Special Resources*.

CARPET: Pick up lint.

All told there were about 20 such lines, and when a task was done, it was initialled in the boxes by the person who did it.

The paper on which the system was printed was tacked to a wall in one of the high traffic backroom areas. Everyone could see what had been completed and the tasks are spread around according to who had time available.

There was one section for the *Start-up Procedures*, a section for the *During-the-Day Procedures* and a section for the *End-of-Day Procedures*.

First CNe (Cont.)

> Still, far from being happy with our efforts, when it was done everyone looked at it glumly. It was a long and daunting list and all to be done before the first client arrived. Where would they find the time!
>
> But, as we got used to the system, it didn't seem to take as long as everyone had thought it would. And as we learned the order of the items and the list was refined, gradually the tasks were done more quickly and with less and less conscious thought and effort.
>
> After a while, preparing the Lounges became so quick and easy that we had time for a cup of tea and a chat before the first person arrived. It was like having someone else doing the work. The customers were impressed and we had our first working CNe!

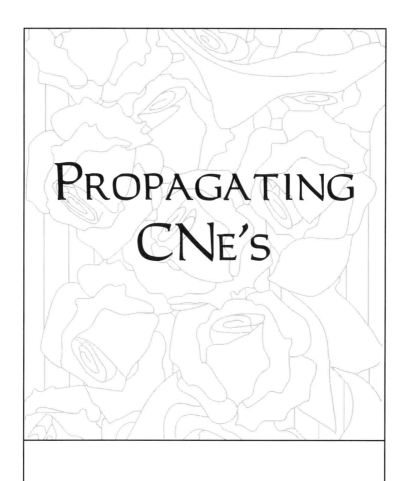

PROPAGATING CNe's

*CNe's are easy to construct – so long as
you understand the rules!*

Propagating CNe's

CNe's are easy to construct – so long
as you understand the rules!

I am sure that you already have some CNe's working in your own business whether or not you understand the rules that you followed to create them.

Most of us have an innate feeling for what works to impress customers and that feeling becomes stronger with experience.

However, if you take the time to consider that there are rules for most things, and that if you follow them life is far easier, then it won't seem too strange to you that CNe construction can be more simple and predictable if you follow a particular path.

Left to yourself to ponder what it is that makes the CNe's tick, I am sure that you would come up with the answers. But perhaps with a few more of my experiences (and those of the not-so-young Inventor) we can speed up the process!

Propagating CNe's

Unfortunately for the Inventor, because he was only working from faded old diagrams, the punch cards that he inserted into the CNe Generator to programme his newly created CNe's were not very acurate.

Sometimes he had to insert them into the machine many times and wait for long periods before the machine was successful in reading them. Sometimes they didn't work at all and sometimes he only produced more nasty Ne's.

Frustrated, the inventor set to decoding the cards and eventually deciphered their contents. What he found when he finished his decoding was that each card represented a series of CNe Propagation Principles.

Card 1: Propagation Principle
Areas outside of the core task at hand are more easily observed and of more obvious benefit to customers.

Card 2: Propagation Principle
Obvious care and attention to detail in the little things creates strong positive impressions of core technical competence.

Card 3: Propagation Principle
Work and effort on these little things is vitally important, and everyone involved must highly value the contribution it makes.

Card 4: Propagation Principle
The effect of efforts in these non-core areas is only as good as the simple consistency with which they are flawlessly completed.

The Inventor's discovery of these simple but powerful principles enabled him to program the generator directly rather than to laboriously push cards into its reader and wait for the machine to decode them.

With his new-found knowledge, it was not long before he had a production line going with CNe's emerging from the generator just like magic!

Propagating CNe's

If you want to create CNe's consistently and easily you have to understand these four principles and how they apply in your business or profession:

Principle 1: Creating Your CNe's

Areas outside of the core task at hand are more easily observed and of more obvious benefit to customers.

Principle 2: Creating Your CNe's

Obvious care and attention to detail in the little things creates strong positive impressions of core technical competence.

For an Electrician

Suppose you are an electrician, and you want people to think you are good at your job.

You know that if customers are not confident in your work they'll imagine all sorts of things that may go wrong — things that may be a danger to themselves or their family.

Not many people take the time to brush up on the SAA Wiring Rules for domestic installations before they call an electrician so most of your customers don't have any idea whether or not you'll follow correct installation standards.

So what could you do to persuade your customers that you have done your job competently?

Well, you could send them to Electricians School for a few years so that they are competent to judge your work. Alternatively you could pay for an independent outside consultant to assess each of your jobs and give your customers a written report.

On the other hand you could make sure: that you were polite and punctual ... that you cleaned up every little bit of wire that you had left on the floor ... and that you removed the finger marks from the walls around where you were working. Your customers, seeing so much unnecessary attention to small details, would be convinced that you pay attention to the bigger things — that your wiring is safe and will be trouble free.

I think either one of these paths would be effective, but the last one — attention to the little details — seems far simpler.

And to automate the process, you could create CNe's for leaving the area where you worked spotless. The system might include a detailed description of the method, a checklist, a system for reporting and a small cleanup toolbox, which could have cleaning cloths, a small vacuum cleaner, a bottle of spray cleaner, rubber gloves etc.

I believe that customers would quite naturally assume, thanks to all the effort you took in the cleanup, that you took at least as much care joining the wires and checking the wiring is properly earthed.

Once you had created your cleanup CNe, it would work tirelessly for you convincing your customers that you were a great electrician.

 PADDI POINTER

A WELL-DESIGNED CNe WILL CONVINCE PEOPLE THAT YOU REALLY ARE AS GOOD AS YOU KNOW YOU ARE!

For a Dental Laboratory

Dental laboratories make the caps, the gold inlays and the bridges that dentists place in customers' mouths. I have dealt with many dental laboratories in my time – some good, some bad.

When I order a cap from a laboratory, I know that it is vital that the cap is the right colour and fits the tooth exactly. To me, the customer, everything else is far less important.

Unfortunately, no cap ever fits perfectly – it's impossible. And no cap is an absolutely perfect colour match. If I look hard enough and long enough through the binocular microscopes I use, I can always find a flaw. I am far more particular than my customers!

Most of these flaws are completely unimportant – they are invisible to the naked eye and do not affect the longevity of the cap in any way. When I look for and find these little imperfections, I often become annoyed with the quality of the laboratory's work.

However, I notice with certain laboratories that I am hypercritical, and with others, I am the reverse. The more I believe in the quality of the laboratory, the less critical I am. The more suspicious I am of the quality, the more closely I look.

Even with my heightened awareness of these matters, you'd think I could look beyond the little things. But I can't.

I am suspicious of the quality of a cap if:

- It arrives at the last minute or late.

- It comes in an old battle-scarred plastic sandwich box.

- The note from the laboratory is dog-eared and scribbled on.

- There is nothing on the note to say that they have followed my precise instructions.

None of these factors has any direct effect on the quality of the cap itself, but they are very important to my eyes none the less. These are the laboratory's critical non-essentials – those things that are not really within the core of their business (making the caps etc.) but which nevertheless have a profound effect on me, their customer.

There are some positive things that the dental laboratory can do to appeal to my emotions and build my trust:

I am a sucker for packaging. If the cap was sealed in a nice box with a little sticker that bore some sort of well designed logo, I would be seduced into feeling that there is quality inside. (Just as I am seduced into feeling that the motel toilet really has been 'cleaned and sealed for my protection' with the little paper band that covers the bowl, when my medical mind knows that really it is still chock-a-block with pathogenic bacteria.)

If the communication from the laboratory is pristine, the writing in careful calligraphy, I would feel the same care has been taken with my cap.

If the cap arrives on or before time, I surmise that since the laboratory has a good delivery system, they probably have good systems for making the cap.

I know that logically these little things do not affect the quality of the cap, but they do help me feel differently about it. And how I think about the quality alters the reverence and care with which I handle the cap. The critical way I regard the cap affects my care in fitting it, and ultimately my job satisfaction ... and my customers satisfaction.

So, if I were running a dental laboratory, I would make CNe's in the areas I mentioned, and I would expect that the satisfaction of my clients would increase markedly.

Principle 3: Creating Your CNe's

Work on these little things is vitally important, and everyone in the team must highly value the contribution it makes.

I hope that after reading thus far you would feel there is a reasonable amount of truth in the following statement:

"Spotlessly clean walls in a business area are the exception rather than the rule. Those who notice — that's not everyone, but certainly more than you realise — will be very impressed. They will be impressed by your attention to detail and will most likely assume that it extends to the core part of your business."

Unfortunately, the people in your organisation who will implement your CNe's may not feel the same way. And the less important they think these tasks, the less likely they are to perform them to perfection.

The way to persuade people to be vigilant and tireless in their creation and maintenance of perfect CNe's is to educate them to the real importance of the seemingly non-essentials.

Be sure that you help everyone in your organisation to understand the 'power of the ordinary'. If you can show your people that it's in their best interest to impress customers ... and that CNe's really wow customers ... then they will labour to make your CNe's work consistently.

Principle 4: Creating Your CNe's

The effect of efforts in these non-core areas is only as good as the simple consistency with which they are flawlessly completed.

Simple Systems

It is silly to do something that requires a lot of effort and brainpower if you don't have to. So design your CNe's around simple routine systems to help you perform them the same way every time, without exceptional effort.

You can't perform consistently without good systems. They have to be easy to use and foolproof, otherwise they quickly fall down. It may be hard to set up the systems initially, but putting work in at the start saves far more time and effort over the long term.

Many of our systems were really hard to create and to perfect. However, now we seem to do them easily, almost without thinking.

If you had told me ten years ago about all the CNe's we now have, I'd have thought you were crazy, that we would be spending all our time getting things ready for customers. Ironically, even with all the extra CNe's we have, I find we are now more productive than we ever have been. We have learned to make simple systems for the CNe's that have a large impact on our customers, and after the initial development stage, they require relatively little effort on our part.

In my mind, that's good business sense.

If your CNe's happen automatically, you and your people will have more time and energy left for the other things that need managing.

92

In our local shopping centre I have seen a very good example of a system for a CNe. It's not very exciting, but it achieves a quietly impressive result. It involves the cleaning of their washrooms.

Washroom

This shopping centre's washrooms are always clean and sparkling. Needless to say, the management have instituted a system for making sure their washrooms are always spick-and-span.

I talked to the head of the centre and she told me of their system.

- The cleaners are given a manual, part of which designates how washrooms are to be cleaned.

- They are trained so that they can perform to the required standard.

- There is a card inside the door of the washroom that indicates the time that the washroom was last cleaned and the person who cleaned it. The card also indicates the time for the next cleaning.

- Patrons are urged to ring the supervisor if the washroom is not clean and a scheduled cleaning is not imminent.

- The supervisor checks periodically to see that the cleaners are doing their job to the required standard and that they are writing up the cards correctly.

- At the end of the week the cards are checked to see that the standard for cleaning frequency has been met.

A system like this is almost foolproof. It is easy to understand and easily followed. It is obvious when it is not being used correctly, and corrective action can be taken quickly. In this way the shopping centre management has systematised their CNe so that it is performed consistently and easily.

I am sure that this impresses both customers and shopkeepers. They see the pristine washrooms and feel that the management is providing a hygienic and caring environment.

Over to you

It is hard to make sure that the little things are always done in a consistent way. To do this necessitates good CNe's. It will take time and effort to make them, but it is time and effort well spent, and you will be rewarded on each occasion your customers are impressed.

And once your entire team realises the importance of these non-core parts of your business, your standards will lift. You will see that things you thought previously unimportant become critical and you'll raise the bar of quality even higher.

THE CNe ADVANTAGE

Cleaning and polishing confirm technical competence!

THE CNE ADVANTAGE

Cleaning and polishing confirm technical competence!

know it's hard to imagine a business system taking on a personality, but that's how I see my CNe's.

I find systems tend to be a bit dull and boring and that is why I've chosen to animate them with a little anthropomorphism. (I admit that I am making a little free and loose with the meaning of the word.)

By representing a system with the illustrations of the CNe characters, even in my own mind, the process of systematising the non-essentials has become more pleasurable. (And things tend to get done in proportion to the pleasure they give.)

I find CNe's to be very co-operative and happy to help around the place. I also find that they are humble about their work. CNe's work behind the scenes and don't like the limelight, unlike their counterparts, the Super CNe's whom you will meet later.

CNe's have a lot of advantages. There is the obvious one about confirming competence. However there are other advantages which are not so obvious ...

The CNe Advantage

The CNe's do their stuff!

A few months after the birth of the first CNe, the Inventor's workplace had changed considerably. The nasty Ne's had all disappeared — the Inventor had recycled them all into brand new CNe's and the little laboratory was far more clean and tidy as a result of their work.

The CNe Generator still stood in the middle of the floor, but it was now pristine and sparkling, though the conveyor was a little worn from constant use.

Now the Inventor had an increase of customers and they seemed to appreciate what he did and respected his talent far more than before. He found himself wryly amused. He knew all these accolades were well-deserved, but he had been just as talented before the arrival of the new CNe's and had nearly starved!

The people in the village saw how useful the Inventor's CNe's were to him, and they asked him to make some that they could use. The Inventor set to work at this task with gusto and soon the whole kingdom was benefiting from the work of the new CNe's. They cleaned off all the years of accumulated grime, and they polished and waxed and dusted until every business was gleaming!

Soon trade improved, and the new-found customers showed a real appreciation of the skills of the artisans and the goods of the traders. The CNe's were having their magical effect.

Customers again came from the nearby kingdoms and principalities. Not nearly as many as in the time of the Master Inventor, but certainly enough to give the land a feeling that prosperity was just around the corner.

AS a result of all the CNe's hard work the people now found their life much easier. They had the respect of their customers and for each other. The whole atmosphere in the Kingdom was lifted.

Employees seemed more proud of their master's goods, they worked better together and they seemed to have more time to stop and chat with their customers.

For the first time in many years, in the Land of the CNe's, you could glimpse people at work actually smiling!

The Inventor was very pleased indeed!

The CNe Advantage

AIDS Aid

A few years ago there was a great furore in the dental community when a number of patients in the United States were infected with the AIDS virus by their dentist. The community was greatly concerned that dentists may not be sterilising their instruments effectively.

From what I heard subsequently, all of the patients concerned shared the same dentist and he had deliberately infected them with his own tainted blood. Patients' concern about the cleanliness of dental instruments may have been a bit undeserved, but for a short while everyone in the dental profession was running scared.

There were newspaper articles and television exposés telling people how dangerous it could be to visit their dentist.

The local Dental Association took the unprecedented step of sending out a poster we could all put up in our waiting rooms to assure patients that dentistry was safe, that the cleanliness of any poster-displaying dentist was as close to godliness as was possible.

In spite of this preventative action, many of my colleagues told me that there was still a great concern among their own patients who continually questioned them about their sterilising techniques. Some dentists I know started tours of their sterilising areas to short circuit the distrust that patients had developed.

In my business, we had no tours and I did not put up the poster. I did type out a description of our sterilising system that I could hand out to inquirers, but nobody inquired and the pages gathered dust in a drawer.

I think it was the CNe's that made our life so easy at this difficult time. Customers saw that we took so much care of the cleanliness of our office and that the tea set and silver were all sparkling so they automatically assumed that we did at least the same for our instruments.

 PADDI POINTER A SPOTLESS TEACUP IS WORTH ALL THE ASSURANCES OF CLEANLINESS THAT CAN BE PRINTED.

Teamwork

CNe's work to impress customers so that they will think highly of the quality in your core business, but CNe's are also happy to work on your staff too.

You might think that team areas (which are out of the customer's eye) do not have a direct impact on customers. However, you will find that quality care in one area will quickly affect the other.

Even if you think your customers are more important than your staff (Myself, I feel my team are more important than customers) you might consider that your team-people have the capacity to influence a great many of your clients.

Your team people also need to believe that your business is a 'good' business. Those who work in a business often have their own area of expertise, and they don't always understand how well the other people in the organisation do their jobs. In this case they act in a similar way to customers: judging peoples competence on the 'little things'. So if you want your team people to respect each other's work and your work, the CNe's can help you.

Crockery Shared

When I first bought fine new Royal Doulton china and silver tea service for my customers, the team and I were all drinking out of plastic cups and using plastic spoons.

Through learning about the CNe's I soon realised that this was counter productive. Plastic made my team feel un-appreciated and eroded their feeling of self worth when what I really wanted was for them to feel appreciated and confident of their ability.

Now we all use the same china and all feel special whenever we have a cup of tea or a dental bun!

If you make sure that your team have the same standard of incidentals as your customers they will know that you care about them and, just as with customers, their estimation of the quality of the business with which they are associated will climb. As an added benefit they are likely to pass on this viewpoint to your customers.

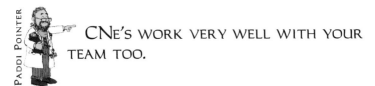

CNe's work very well with your team too.

CNe's and Rugby Unions Football

The game of Rugby Union is a tough physical game, sometimes brutal in its punishment of the players, and is notorious for its no-complaining, testosterone-fuelled camaraderie. On the field and off players are known more for their brawn and cauliflower ears than the elegance of their dress. They act tough and they are treated roughly! I have met few rugby veterans without some sort of permanent injury gained in the scrum, ruck and maul of this no-quarter-given sport.

In England not too many years ago, the situation wasn't much different.

However, with his appointment as head coach of the England Rugby Union Team, Clive Woodward changed all that. At the time, the England team were doing really badly. It was his job to turn them around. But Clive is a visionary and he didn't just want to show his team how to be winners, Clive wanted, as he put it, to completely change the face of England Rugby.

Clive visited me in Australia a few months before taking the national coaching job. He was particularly taken by my concept of the Critical Non-essentials — which proves he is a bit unusual because lots of business people up to that point thought it was a little crazy — and eventually this was one of the tools he used in his new position.

The transformation of England Rugby

For Clive, everything started with his players. He wanted to create an experience for them that would instil a strong sense of pride in the team and the feeling that they were a valuable part of something far more wonderful than they had ever imagined possible. The Critical Non-essentials became one of the key factors in creating this 'winning' mindset.

As well as working on the skills and tactics of the team, they created many systems that had little to do with the core activity: coaching and playing rugby.

Clive and his management team did everything in their power to make CNe's that completely set them apart from their major competitors, the Australian Wallabies, New Zealand All Blacks and South African Springboks.

For example, the English National team had been used to staying in cheap accommodation and arriving at matches in tatty coaches. Now, instead of motels, twin share rooms and training camp huts as before, Clive arranged for his world-class players to stay in world-class accommodation. Players each had five-star rooms with personalised name plates on their door and Clive even arranged for framed action photographs of each player for their room.

There was the problem of unreliable, inconsistent transportation, buses that often were too small to carry the whole team and which would arrive late or break down just before test matches. Clive solved this by convincing a coach hire company to outfit a brand new coach in England Rugby colours and insignia and dedicated that bus solely to the team's activities. Now the players arrived for their matches in pristine coaches rather than the buses they had previously packed into.

The Change Rooms at Twickenham, England's home stadium, transformed from bare block walls into a colourful, inspirational 'Home of Champions'.

Uniforms were completely redesigned with special fabric to make players harder to tackle, and everyone was given a fresh set of kit to put on at half time so they started the second half with the right mindset. The dress kit for official functions was sourced from the finest tailors in London.

Certainly all this cost money and it was money that might otherwise have been used on more core training areas, but these non-essentials had everything to do with how their players perceived themselves and their worth and greatly affected their attitudes, energy and commitment on the pitch.

Clive and his management team were able to demand more from their players than they had ever known they could give. The CNe's helped the squad feel that they were a part of a winning team, and by all accounts they performed accordingly.

Over his seven years as coach, Clive and his management team created hundreds of critical non-essentials that helped them totally redefine what it meant for players to pull on the white England jersey.

Clive's team won the Rugby World Cup now Clive is 'Sir Clive' — what a winner!

As Clive proved, CNe's aren't just an effective tool for use with customers in service situations. They too can have a dramatic impact on how any team feel about their work environment. And on a more mundane note, CNe's can also work their magic on your suppliers.

New Building

> When I built my new building I was very picky — almost hyper-critical. I worried about the little details precisely because I was starting to realise that the little details affected the big things.
>
> For the first few weeks I was continually checking the quality of work and making sure that we always supplied the trades-people with a cool drink or a cup of tea. I wanted them to feel that we all cared about what they were doing.
>
> Each night I would make sure that the floors were cleaned of dust and debris so that the workers had a clean start in the morning.
>
> Pretty soon the trades-people started to clean up themselves and pay more attention to detail. They felt that they were working on a quality building and this influenced them to pay more attention to the quality of their work.
>
> New trades-people saw the quality of work done by the trades who came before and made sure what they did was up to scratch.
>
> Now, a few years on I still have people in the building trade who comment on how well my building is constructed and surmise that I must know a lot about building (which I don't).

If you start off well and look after the little things, people will do the 'right thing'. Start off badly and everyone follows suit.

You only have to watch the progressive wrecking of a car that has been parked in a lonely place to realise this. The car can sit for a few days with no damage. But once someone steals just one wheel, the rest of the car is stripped in no time at all. It can become a wreck in a matter of hours. Once something degenerates, people lose their respect for it.

If one person lays a brick wrongly and it is not corrected, the rest of the trades-people will assume that the builder does not care. Do one thing well and others are done well.

CONCENTRATE ON THE LITTLE THINGS IN BUSINESS AND THE BIG THINGS TEND TO LOOK AFTER THEMSELVES.

Ancient Roman CNe's

In war as in business, the incidentals have a great power to change people's perceptions. And it's been that way for a long time ...

When they saw the ancient Roman army lined up, all gleaming metal and honed spears, the barbarians on the fringes of the empire must have quaked in their tatty boots.

The reputation of the Roman soldiers went before them: they were formidable fighters. How much this reputation must have been enhanced when the opposition saw their obsessive attention to detail in things which didn't seem to matter: they marched in line, cleaned their boots and even had their hair cut!

That the Legionaries put so much time into the incidentals was an indication to the raggle-taggle troops facing them that the Romans must have spent even more time on the skills of fighting and the art of war.

No wonder the Romans won their battles with such monotonous regularity!

CNe's CAN SERVE TO INTIMIDATE YOUR OPPOSITION BY INFLUENCING THEIR MINDSET.

The Efficiency of CNe's!

You might find that the CNe's characters look simple and comical, but I have learned that their appearance belies their power and efficiency and they are great illustrations of the above examples.

Fellowship Ignored

I spent a good few years working on my dental Fellowship. Some of that time returned a benefit to me because I have become more skilled than I had been. However, a large part of the reason I wanted this extra qualification was that I wanted my customers to be impressed.

And so they are – but not much!

A few of my customers do feel I am somewhat more skilled and slightly better qualified than my peers just because I have an extra certificate hanging on the wall. However most don't notice it at all and even if I point it out to them they seem less impressed than they are with the certificate I have for attending an implant course which took me all of three days but is bigger and more brightly coloured!

The only thing that stops me grinding my teeth into dust on these occasions is the realisation that customers do think me more competent and skilled than average, and it is because of my efforts. Just not those in formal education, because for the most part, it's the time and effort I have spent on my CNe's that confirm my competence.

They look at my Certificate and think, "Ho-hum," but they see the sparkle of the silver in the tea service and they think "Wow! He must be good!"

Certainly, I have put effort into making my CNe's: devising them, modifying and systematising them, but not half as much as I put into my Fellowship qualification. No, my CNe's have been far more efficient in terms of results for effort.

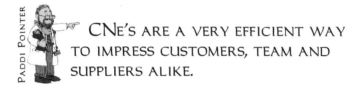

CNE'S ARE A VERY EFFICIENT WAY TO IMPRESS CUSTOMERS, TEAM AND SUPPLIERS ALIKE.

Bringing out the best

One of my CNe's involves the gardens that surround the front of our building.

Well-kept Gardens

In the gardens that front my building there are a variety of tropical and subtropical plants that give the building a happy appearance and a dozen or so topiary trees whose manicured precision frames the building well.

I feel that tidy and well-kept gardens are important because they give my customers their first impressions of my business.

When the gardens were first landscaped, there were lots of people who said that they would be quickly vandalised. As it turned out, we have had very little destruction.

I am still not sure whether it's because intending vandals don't want to damage such a beautiful area or because so many people pass by and look at the gardens that anyone misbehaving would be easily spotted. For whatever reason, we have had little trouble when all around there was graffiti and vandalism.

Since we put in our pleasant little gardens, other buildings on either side of us have done so as well and now they suffer less damage too. The whole street has improved!

A GOOD CNe HAS A POSITIVE EFFECT ON EVERYONE.

Well-kept Gardens (II)

Richard maintains our gardens and he does an excellent job. However, it worried me that Richard came only once every two weeks.

Gardens in Queensland grow so rapidly, that our topiary trees started to look tatty just a few days after he had clipped them, and weeds came up overnight.

I did not want to pay for Richard to come more often, so to solve the problem, I suggested that he put a small plaque on the wall at the front of the garden where it could be easily read by anyone walking past.

The plaque says that it is Richard who maintains the gardens and it gives the telephone number for people to ring him.

The garden is now always pristine, in spite of the fact that I have not increased Richard's hours of work. I am sure that to Richard keeping our gardens perfect is good advertising and now I often see him stop by just to check that nothing is out of place.

Richard tells me that he gets a lot of business from people who drive by and admire his work in our gardens. This knowledge leads him to take great care when tending to our plants. For Richard taking care of the little things is good for his business, and it's good for ours too!

Other people's Cne's can work for you!

So, by all means make your CNe's to impress your customers and convince them of your competence in your chosen field. However, don't forget that there are many other CNe advantages that you may not immediately recognise!

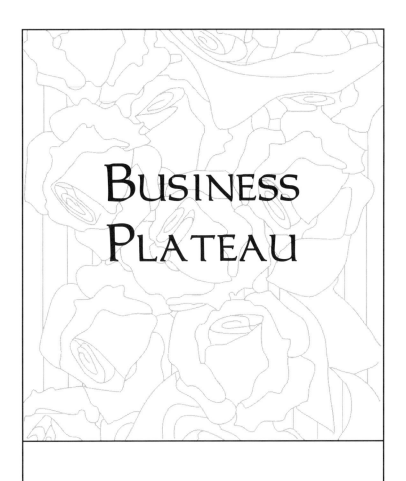

BUSINESS PLATEAU

An aura of competence alone is not enough for success.

BUSINESS PLATEAU

*An aura of competence alone is not
enough for success.*

f you are good at what you do and have taken
care of the incidentals so that your customers
realise you are competent, then you probably
have a reasonable business that has been growing modestly
over the years.

However, if you depend on this belief in your competence
as your main source of new customers, your business
probably has never grown as quickly as you might have
hoped, and at some point has likely reached a plateau.

If you want a constant stream of good new customers you
have to conduct more than merely adequate business —
there has to be some magic in what you do, something that
makes your customers think:

"Wow! That was a great experience! How did they do
that?"

Business Plateau

Business had certainly improved for the people in the Land of the CNe's, but not nearly enough. There were still debts to pay from the lean times, and though the customers who came seemed far happier than before, there were not enough of them.

Hearing of the problem with customer numbers, the King, who had become far more interested in the kingdom's commerce since the recent improvements, organised a meeting in the Great Hall at the palace to look for solutions.

Soon the whole room was buzzing with ideas to make the kingdom's businesses better known. "We could advertise on the castle walls," suggested the butcher.

"We could sponsor troubadours to visit neighbouring kingdoms to tell about our wares" was the idea of the candle-maker. "Those fellows really have the gift of the gab!"

"We could hire a scribe to write glowing letters about our businesses and hand them out on the major highroads of the neighbouring kingdoms. It would be costly, but I am sure it would be worth it," said the local sheriff.

However, as the Baker pointed out, those sorts of things were already being done by bards and scribes and troubadours employed by the merchants in the surrounding lands.

And as the mercer observed, most people were so heartily sick of false promises and self-serving stories that rather than patronise business that did this crowing, they tended to avoid them!

No one wanted to cause that sort of reaction but what else could they do to reach prospective customers?

───────────

Business Plateau

I found my business was stagnating. I was working harder to find new customers and yet I was acquiring fewer.

No matter how well I did the core part of my work — and the non-essential parts too — I didn't have enough new work coming in to keep growing. After a certain point, trying to improve my lot was like walking through treacle, and I was anxious for an answer to my predicament of exhaustive hard work with seemingly little more to show for it.

Advertising

During the 70's and 80's the public face of dentistry in Australia changed a lot.

Previously the profession had been quite reclusive. There was lots of work for everyone and so no one worried about advertising for new customers.

With the advent of fluoridated water, toothpastes and the reduction of sugar intake, people's teeth got better and better. There was no longer a queue of people wanting treatment lining up at my front door!

To remedy this problem, the wisdom of the time said, "Use marketing and advertising." The main thrust of this was:

- Put your name out in front of the public. Advertise that you are gentle, caring, and have personable staff.

- Be available for emergencies 24 hours in the day. See lots of people with toothache in the dead of night.

If you do this, people will be grateful and will become good customers. Persist, and pretty soon you will have lots of new customers.

I tried it!

24hr Dentist

> I was the 24 hr dentist. I had lots of new customers for my after hours service, but sometimes I would be at my surgery three times in a night. I was frazzled, but I consoled myself with the fact that I was building my business.
>
> It was not till I got my first computer and was able to generate some good financial reports that I realised the awful truth!
>
> All those people that I spent so much time seeing in the dead of night actually cost me money. Not only did they rarely become long-tem customers after I had cured their pain, but they regularly failed to pay their bills!

Most of those who had toothache and needed to be seen at strange hours were disorganised people.

Occasionally there was someone who had an unforeseen problem but mostly I was seeing people who had suffered discomfort for months before they rang me. They lurched from crisis to crisis in their lives and they went for the quick fix.

My speciality was treating discriminating people who wanted a high standard of care in keeping with my training. These emergency customers rarely fell into that category.

And the story I was consequently encouraging them to tell their friends of my practice was basically this: "If you have a problem, don't worry about it. Paddi Lund will get up at any time of the night to fix it for you so you might as well wait until it's really bad."

116

After a time, I realised I wanted a different kind of story told of me by a different kind of customer.

And this I discovered was the main problem with any advertising I undertook. There was no question that advertising brought in new customers. Unfortunately, it attracted many people who didn't really fit my perception of the ideal.

This would not be a problem for a low overhead business, where you just get rid of any people you don't want or need. But for me it cost large amounts of money and lost productive time every time I did a case workup and presentation on a customer who didn't really want what I was offering in the first place. It was very frustrating. And in a society that was becoming increasingly litigious it was becoming dangerous to have customers with whom I was not completely compatible.

The concept of 'Avocation'

Luckily, about this time I began to explore the power of avocation in business:

"When someone else says nice things about you it is far more powerful than if you say it yourself."

The logic behind avocation is this:

"When you say nice things about yourself it sounds self serving and improbable, but when someone else praises you it provides an independent and more trustworthy value judgement."

Compounded by Frustration

I really didn't want my professional life to be so hard. It was a strain, constantly working to find new customers. And I wanted lots of really great customers: A-class customers, customers who wanted exactly what I wanted them to have and didn't quibble over the prices. (Call me naive! No one told me how silly and idealistically impossible that would sound to normal business people!)

In addition, in a fit of professional pride, I decided I wanted my customers to feel that they were privileged to be under my care, rather than the other way around, which was prevalent: my customers seemed to take the view that I should be grateful for their patronisation. I was always on the back foot, and as a professional trying to create a position of expertise, that just didn't work well for me.

This concept of 'Avocation' and the 'Word-of-mouth' advertising that it logically led to went a long way towards solving my problem of finding an adequate number of good new customers who wanted what I had to offer.

From Competent to Expert

While an understanding of the power of the CNe's had enabled me to help clients feel that I was competent at what I did, unfortunately that had not been enough to attract an adequate flow of good new customers.

However, it occurred to me that if customers thought I was offering something out of the ordinary, perhaps they would consequently encourage their friends to see me.

I knew that I wasn't the best dentist around — the best technical dentists usually worked in universities because they could not make it in the real world. Just being the best is no guarantee that customers will think you the best. I felt that I needed a new type of CNe to sing my praises.

The CNe's gave people an additional story to tell about me. It was, "That Dr Lund is competent at what he does and he runs a tight ship". Not a bad story, but not good enough to capture people's attention at a dinner party.

It was fine to be recognised as competent and proficient at what I did, certainly, but that wasn't enough to make for a great tale. What I needed was a new, exciting and interesting account that people could tell to their friends.

But how could I generate a story like that?

Well, that's where the Super-CNe's came in ...

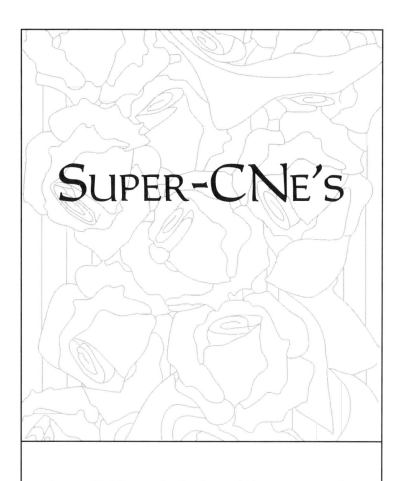

SUPER-CNE'S

Super-CNe's supply the 'Wow' that gives people a great story to tell about your business.

SUPER-CNE'S

---

*Super-CNe's supply the 'Wow' that
gives people a great story to tell about
your business*

he stories that people tell about your business
are very important. Especially so when you
realise that they tend to be of two types: very
positive and very negative.

There are very few in-between business stories because not
many people would bother telling a tale about something
so banal. For instance you don't often hear:

- "I bought a fridge the other day and the people
  who served me were reasonably polite and gave me
  adequate service."

- "I went to a cricket match and it wasn't too
  boring."

- "I went to the dentist and it was ok — not too
  painful..."

These are uninteresting stories. They would not generate
much kudos for the teller, so why would anyone bother?

No, what people are looking for are juicy stories to tell,
and that is where the Super CNe's come in ...

Super-CNe's

After listening to the marketing problems with which the people were wrestling, the Inventor again toiled at his drafting board and eventually he came up with a design for a new high-powered CNe that he felt might help.

It was a long shot, but perhaps this new 'Super-CNe' could help generate the great publicity for which the kingdom yearned?

And so, one afternoon when all was in readiness, the Inventor approached the CNe Generator, punched buttons and twiddled at dials, studied his clipboard one final time and pulled down the Master Switch.

The little CNe's clustered around the machine as it hummed and gently vibrated. Lights flashed and the conveyor started up, no longer with a 'clack' but, thanks to the continued maintenance by the CNe's, with a well-oiled *whirrrr*.

A striking figure, somewhat larger than the Generator's previous progeny, appeared in the machine's portal and was carried forward by the conveyor. It stepped on to the laboratory floor, smiled broadly and flexed its muscles – the first Super-CNe!

The Inventor joined hands with the new-born being and together with the other little CNe's who were gathered round, they all danced excitedly together.

The Super-CNe set to work and soon it was creating systems and events that gave customers exciting stories to tell about the Inventor and his work. And just as planned, these customers immediately rushed off to tell their friends these exciting tales of their experience!

Super-CNe's I
First Creations

It is vital to any business that people talk in a positive way about it. The usual method for achieving this is through advertising.

Unfortunately, people are often jaded from hearing and seeing too many self-serving messages. They are cynical from years of lies and half-truths, and much advertising is often seen by customers as a business blowing its own trumpet ... sometimes very badly!

Before the development of written language and mass media, word-of-mouth was essential to the spreading of knowledge and ideas. Even today, and in spite of all the modern technology we have, the spoken word remains very powerful and remarkably speedy. Moreover, because it is based on the trust generated between individuals, word-of-mouth communication has a believable quality that advertising often lacks.

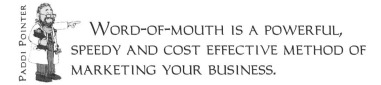

WORD-OF-MOUTH IS A POWERFUL, SPEEDY AND COST EFFECTIVE METHOD OF MARKETING YOUR BUSINESS.

Super-CNe's engineer word-of-mouth advertising by persuading uninvolved third parties to say nice things about your business. To illustrate, please let me tell you the story of Joe Manzini, a fictitious plumber, and I think you will quickly get the idea of the potential of these special CNe's.

125

Joe the (Fictitious) Plumber

There once was a plumber whose name was Joe Manzini. He could weld water pipes very, very well. He had the finest welding equipment, and used the most expensive brazing rods. And he had been to special courses so that he could weld faster and more accurately than any of his competitors.

He was very excited about his skill because he saw it as a way of creating a good impression on his customers. His fellow plumbers were certainly very impressed with his expertise. They had given him a special *Award for Plumbing Excellence* on numerous occasions and he was often called on to talk at the *Plumbing Circle* dinners.

Strangely, his welding skills didn't seem to be as exciting to his customers as they were to his fellow plumbers. His customers didn't seem overcome with admiration when they saw his immaculate pipe -joins. And he didn't get <u>any</u> new customers ringing up saying things like:

"Is that Joe Manzini? Well, my friend was telling me all about your lovely joins and the fact that you're the best person in town for welding pipes..."

Nothing at all like that. It just didn't seem fair to Joe that he had gone to all the trouble of honing his skills and the very people he needed to impress remained disappointingly unimpressed! In spite of all his plumbing skills, Joe's business was not going so well.

After much thought Joe decided that he would have to do something very different if he wanted his customers to talk about him and give good recommendations to their friends — but just what it was he should do quite eluded him.

It so happened that one night, while he was on his way to that year's Plumbing Banquet, where he was to receive another award for plumbing excellence, he answered an emergency telephone call from an old lady: "Leaking pipe, need help, come quick!"

Much to his wife's chagrin, Joe, being a kind soul, decided to answer the distress call, and, still in his dinner suit, he performed to his normal level of excellence and quickly dealt with the lady's leak. His customer seemed more impressed than was usual and Joe received a thank-you note. (This was very unusual.) Even more unusual still, over the next few weeks Joe received a number of calls from people referred by the lady customer he had helped out.

When Joe went out to do some work for the first of these new customers, Mrs Zog, this good lady seemed very happy with the repair that Joe did for her, but she expressed disappointment that he was not wearing his usual 'plumbing uniform'. (You can imagine the tale Mrs Zog had been told!)

Perplexed, it wasn't until a similar experience at the home of his second referred customer that Joe began to catch on. Happy to play right along, from that time he decided try going to work in a black dinner suit with a flower in the buttonhole. He became known as the 'sophisticated plumber' and his business boomed.

Sometimes, like for Joe, Super-CNe's come about by accident. Unfortunately, back in the real world, no happy accidents befell me, and I still had a bit to learn before I my first Super-CNe went to work.

Learning from George (George III)

As you've read, George, my receptionist, entertained patients with his witty conversation and endless cups of tea. I thought it strange to be offering refreshment to customers. *They are only here to have their teeth done*, I would think. After all, we were selling dentistry, not companionship!

Perhaps it's unethical, too? What would my friends at the dental study group think? However, I didn't say anything to George about my doubts, because I had noticed that customers thus entertained complained less and seemed more relaxed and easy to 'work on'.

It was only gradually that I realised the power of the refreshment that George provided. I didn't immediately turn into a tea-swilling dentist, the cappuccino-king-of-the-gnashers I later became, but I did start to do a few little things for our customers entertainment.

One such thing was the provision of a video game for the children. Another was throwing out the tatty old out-of-date magazines in our reception lounge and replacing them with expensive books on art and tea. I also installed a high fidelity sound system in every room and piped carefully selected music, 'Sounds of Nature', through the building. I put TV's in the surgeries for customers to watch during treatment.

At the time, I was not following a coherent strategy. However, there was an incident that made me happy to go further down this path and systematise the whole process of generating great stories for my customers to tell.

Shopping Centre

I was in a shopping centre when I happened to overhear a conversation. One lady was talking animatedly with another. She was telling a good story — you know that when the other party pays rapt attention. What was especially interesting to me was that they were talking about 'Yours-Truly'.

"That Dr Lund, you know, over behind the shops," said the lady telling the story. "Doris said that he's got a lovely place. And do you know what?" (The story teller paused for dramatic effect.) "I know you won't believe it, but THEY HAVE TV's ON THE CEILING!!!"

At this revelation the listener expressed some incredulity because this was at a time when TV was far less common than it is today. The idea that a dentist would provide that sort of luxury for his clientele was almost unbelievable to hear.

The story-telling lady was greatly rewarded by her friend's reaction, and I am sure that she retold the story whenever she could be sure of an appreciative audience.

Afterwards, considering this incident, I thought to myself, *Everyone likes a colourful tale. Why not create some more for my customers to relate to their friends?* So I adapted George's idea of the tea and entertainment, and by taking it a bit further, I made it into a very interesting story.

Tea Culture

> With my heart in my mouth and my hand in my wallet, I purchased a very expensive set of Royal Doulton fine bone china. We started to serve our clients their tea in this fancy service, on a silver tray, with a silver tea strainer and silver spoons. The tea that we used was the best we could purchase, and we bought it in small packets (which are even more expensive) so that it was always fresh. After a short time, we were allowing our clients a choice of 25 regular teas and 15 herbal varieties — a lot of stock.
>
> When sitting with a client I would make a point of stopping our conversation and waiting in silence for a few moments to watch whoever was serving us perform the 'Tea Ceremony' — milk poured carefully in to the cup, tea-pot rotated clockwise three times, careful straining of the ambrosia and a gentle stir of the amber liquid in the tea-cup. It made a good story for customers to tell: the idea of an elegant 'Tea Ceremony' in an otherwise regular 'dental' environment.

The perceived level of service certainly was great, however you've probably realised, all this attention took time. Not to mention that the implements and consumables cost far more than the mug and tea bag that we had previously offered.

So, understandably, whenever I talk to groups of business people about the way we serve tea, there are always a number of people concerned about the cost. My answer is to tell a story:

The X-ray and the Tea Set

It was hard for me to spend nearly a thousand dollars on crockery, and at least as much on the other parts of the tea system. I was worried that I was making a poor business decision. And yet, looking back, I now consider it one of the best investments I have ever made.

In my practice I have an expensive panoramic X-ray machine. It is an impressive looking apparatus, and it produces a remarkably useful x-ray picture. Unfortunately, in all the time that I've had this machine, I haven't ever heard anyone comment on how wonderful it was to have an X-ray with this device.

On the other hand, our crockery, the tea and the tea ceremony have generated any number of positive comments. Clients remark to us (and more importantly their friends) how wonderful it is to have their tea served so elegantly.

The X-ray machine cost $35,000. Each tea set costs under $1000. It seems to me that, as a method of satisfying clients and promoting public relations for my business, the tea set is a much better investment than the X-ray machine.

I figure that over the years the expense of my tea paraphernalia has been returned to me hundredfold in referrals — the X-ray machine has barely broken even.

The Tea Ceremony was my first true Super-CNe. Its story-creating potential convinced me that this was an excellent path to follow. Flush with success, I decided to venture into more exotic areas for my next Super-CNe.

The Count of Cappuccino

I have always wanted to have my own café style espresso machine. So one day I bought one.

Not one of those little domestic models that everyone seems to have nowadays, but one of the real big Italian coffee-lounge varieties, excessively large and gleaming, the 4-Door, V8 muscle-car of Cappuccino Machines.

And I didn't want one of the new push button ones, even though they make the coffee in half the time. I wanted it to have long handles that you pull down to express the coffee. The ones that go, SSSHHHEEEEWWW!!!

I had to order my machine especially from Italy because the distributors weren't importing the models with the handles any more. Most people wanted automation. I was happy to wait, just as long as I got the kind with the handles.

If I had been in the Coffee Shop business, I would probably have opted for efficiency and have kept everything as simple and compact as possible. But seeing that I was in the dental business, the purpose of my espresso machine was quite different.

I wanted coffee making to become a piece of theatre so that having a coffee became an event for my customers and give them a great story to tell of me, the dentist, pulling down on the big handles shrouded by clouds of steam. It would be the icing on the cake of their dental-coffee story!

After months of anticipation, the machine finally arrived. It was everything I wanted it to be. I sat it on a bench just inside the front door, and we scripted a little bit of theatre around it just as we had with the Tea Ceremony. That's where it still is today, where everyone can see it. In its brooding copper-plated magnificence, it never fails to capture a customer's attention.

The Difference between CNe's and Super-CNe's

So now we had CNe's and Super-CNe's.

I must admit that at first I was a little confused regarding the difference. It is only looking back now that I can see the distinction between them clearly. They are similar, but really they serve quite different purposes.

The CNe's do the little 'household' tasks that give customers a reason to believe in the parts of your business they don't fully understand or appreciate. CNe's are not something that clients particularly remember or talk about. They are somewhat in the background — important nevertheless, but not exciting.

The Super-CNe's are CNe's taken to a sensational degree so that everyone remembers and talks about them.

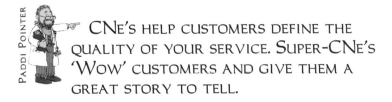

CNE'S HELP CUSTOMERS DEFINE THE QUALITY OF YOUR SERVICE. SUPER-CNE'S 'WOW' CUSTOMERS AND GIVE THEM A GREAT STORY TO TELL.

The Referral Dialogue

But where do ability and quality fit into all of this?

You'll remember Joe the Plumber. Was his success simply due to the fact that he had given people a good story to tell? Wasn't his considerable skill important at all?

Of course it was. Customers are not silly. But before he could show his skill to a new customer, Joe needed to get his current customers to talk about his business and recommend him to others.

Think for a moment about the words you use when you talk favourably about another business. I imagine the conversation about Joe's business might have gone something like this:

"My Plumber, Joe Manzini, always wears a dinner suit and a red carnation. That's right! He does his plumbing in a dinner suit. You should give him a try!"

"Sure, but does he do the plumbing well?" asks the friend.

"Yes, he's a great plumber. Arrives on time, and I never have any problems with leaks or anything, and he always tidies up."

"Oh", says the friend, "I might give him a go."

Joe's Super-CNe's (red carnation and dinner jacket) would get him talked about. His regular CNe's (arrives on time, no problems with the plumbing and he tidies up) would get him new customers and his plumbing skill would keep them.

So, when your customers tell the story of your business, relating your Super-CNe's, the conversation would go something like, "I go to the XYZ business, and you would not believe what they do! They …"

Most people listen interestedly to the Super-CNe story and then give this sort of response, "Yes, but are they good at their job?"

Your customer, who has been talking very positively about your business, will then tend to continue on in this same positive vein to persuade the friend to believe how good you are at your job – otherwise their story would be spoiled.

So, you can see that Super-Cne's give people not only an interesting story to tell, but these people also tend to wax lyrical about the quality of your business. And as well as creating opportunities for word-of-mouth advertising, Super-CNe's can be used in a more mainstream way for publicity.

Public Relations Boon

Since creating my Super CNe's, you'd be amazed at the number of people who have written articles or spoken in audiences about my business. Mostly they talk about my Tea Set, Cappuccino Machine and Dental Buns – three of my Super-CNe's, and items that are, by my design, unusual in a dental business.

And although most have not sampled my dental skills, the speakers or authors of these articles invariably go out of their way to communicate that I am a 'great dentist'. Even for professionals and business authorities, it is hard to say great things about one part of a business and then talk negatively about another.

Super-CNe Logic

Don't be surprised if you find that people's reactions to your Super-CNe's aren't always entirely logical. Super-CNe's have a way of catching people at an emotional level which is far more persuasive than any reasoned thought.

Once, I was consulting with a dentist and his office manager, Wendy. We were discussing CNe's and Super-CNe's when Wendy related the following incident:

The Grandmother's Ophthalmologist

"My grandmother had been having trouble seeing, so I recommended her to go and see an ophthalmologist whom I had heard was very good. My grandmother trusted my judgment in these things so she made an appointment to have her eyes examined and to find out if her very poor vision could be improved.

"Grandmother attended for the examination which took about an hour and a half — far longer than she had expected. It was past lunch time and my grandmother had not had much breakfast so one of the ophthalmologist's staff kindly made her a sandwich. She was overwhelmed by this generosity, and afterwards my grandmother could not stop talking about her visit.

"She kept telling her friends to go and see this wonderful doctor. She told anyone who could be persuaded to listen to her how thorough his examination was. (*It must have been, because he took an hour and a half.*) She swore that he was a really good doctor (*though she knew nothing of the technicalities of medicine*) and that he really cared about her." (*He must care because the staff had worried about her enough to make her a sandwich.*)

Wendy said her grandmother couldn't stop thanking her for recommending this particular ophthalmologist. Wendy was a little embarrassed. "She's always thanking me and I feel a little guilty. After all, in spite of all his treatment, <u>she's still blind as a bat!</u>"

Now Wendy wasn't really describing a Super-CNe about 'sandwiches and hungry elderly ladies'. I am sure the Ophthalmologist had not followed the program steps and systematised a Super-CNe or even recognised its power. It was probably just a 'one off' event. But how well this incident shows the power of doing something warm and personal, beyond the call of duty – and that is the very stuff of Super-CNe's.

Super-CNe's II
Doing It Yourself

Creating your own Super-CNe's

In our last visit to the Land of the CNe's, the Inventor devised a series of programs for his CNe Generator which produced his first Super-CNe. He developed these programs over the years, and you might find his work useful if you want to make fully-functioning Super-CNe's for your own business. The Inventor has kindly given us permission to reproduce them here for your benefit!

Step 1: Creating Super CNe's

Choose an area of interest that you really enjoy.

Most importantly, your Super-CNe's should be enjoyable for you and your team. When they are, there will be a far greater chance that they will be performed well and with some flair.

Baroque Music

One of my Super-CNe's involves Baroque music — it's essentially a particular era of classical music mostly from the 17th and 18th centuries. I wouldn't say it is a particularly well-developed Super-CNe — we have not spent a lot of time taking it to the extreme. At the moment it consists of the following:

- We play only Baroque classical music in the building.

- I have installed a great audio system so that it sounds impressive even to those who do not like this type of music.

- When a particular piece of music plays, we are familiar enough with it to describe the composer and name of the tune to our customers.

- Occasionally, I will give away one of our CD's to customers who like a particular track.

See, I told you it wasn't well developed! However, I can see us extending this Super-CNe so that it becomes a real talking point for our customers. Here is how I see it evolving:

- We will have a description of the 'Today's Recital' displayed in each lounge.

- We will have pictures of Baroque composers and their life stories framed on the walls.

- We will have a composer of the month.

Copy Discriminately

Anyway, the important point about Baroque music in this context is that everyone in my work-family enjoys it. Baroque is one of the few points of commonality in musical taste. Not all of us enjoy Pop, and not all of us like Rap, and not all of us appreciate Big Band ... but we all like Baroque.

If, for instance, we had focussed developing a particular Super-CNe that involved easy-listening music (elevator music), none of us would have enjoyed taking it to the extreme to make a Super-CNe.

Certainly if we wanted to we could have built on elevator music to make a Super-CNe. We could have made our

Clients Personal Lounges look like elevators, and by performing free lobotomies we could have made it so the customer could sit for long periods exposed to these melodies. But I would have felt bad each time a customer talked about my musical taste ... and we would all have gone mad from an overdose of the banal!

Whereas with Baroque music as our Super-CNe, we can all enjoy it and be excited about taking it to the extreme (teasing customers who don't know Bach's birth-date for instance).

Some people, however, could use easy listening as their Super-CNe — and enjoy it. Its horses for courses!

Don't copy someone else's Super-CNe just because it works well for them. Copy discriminately. If it fits in with the tastes of your Business-Family and your culture, then possibly it will work for you. If it doesn't, then it could become more trouble to you than it is worth.

No matter how well it works in another business, if a particular Super-CNe feels uncomfortable for your team, then your customers will sense this and it will not be very successful.

Step 2: Creating Super CNe's

Choose an area that is distant (but not too distant) from the core of your business.

Focus on objects or tasks that seem distant from your core products, services and skills of your business or profession. Why? Because that's what makes the Super-CNe so memorable. However, Super-CNe's must have some relationship to the core of your business otherwise the story they tell will not tend to lead people to say great things about you and what you do.

A Super-CNe should be seen as something that you don't really have to do as part of your regular business. Thus it is seen as 'beyond the call of duty'. Something you do not have to do, but you do anyway. And when you do it with a flare that is dazzling, it will give your customers a great story to tell.

In the early 1990's I had a part in a business video program called *Towards Awesome Service*, produced by Paul Dunn of Results Accountants Systems. Basically, Paul and I sat in a couple of armchairs while drinking tea for an hour or so, chatting about customer service. It was quite unrehearsed.

At one point we were discussing the importance of the 'little things' in business. I described a hypothetical Super-CNe for a steel fabrication business. I would like to return to that imaginary setting to say a little more about how that might work.

The Wonderful Steel Fabrication Company

The management of *Wonderful Steel Fabrication Company* was looking for ways to promote their business. The CEO felt that customers did not find his business very interesting and that this impacted badly on the referral of new customers.

So he brought his people together, and they brainstormed and came up with a few ideas to make doing business more exciting for their clientele. Their best idea had to do with picnics, and with a little work, it evolved into 'picnic hampers'.

With each order of steel over $5000, the company decided to deliver a full picnic hamper to the work-site. They conjectured that getting a delivery of steel is not very exciting but including the gift of a picnic hamper loaded with food would make the delivery greatly anticipated by all. Imagine the scene when the steel was delivered to the building site. Everyone would be excited to see what was in the hamper. Fresh cut sandwiches, biscuits, fruit and soft drinks. It would be shared out for lunch or afternoon tea.

The customer's employees would talk about the hamper for days. They would certainly tell their boss that they were happy with the arrangement and would suggest they deal with *Wonderful Steel Fabrication Company* next time they needed steel products. And they would tell their friends who worked in other businesses that required steel fabrication to order from this company and get a hamper.

The customer's employees would probably try to work out ways that they could turn small orders into big ones – over the magical $5000. (And that would be very advantageous for the *Wonderful Steel Fabrication Company*.)

If the WSFC did this sort of thing on a regular basis, they could get the hampers labelled with their company logo. If the basket was of good enough quality, it would be used by someone in the customer's business time and time again – a continuing piece of promotion.

Under the guidelines of conventional business wisdom, The *Wonderful Steel Fabrication Company* might have decided to promote business by giving away free steel with each order over $5000. This approach may have caused some temporary increase in sales, but it would not have been much talked about. The promotion would have been quickly forgotten because there is nothing very exciting about a gift of steel. The same is true of a discount. Discounts are not memorable and so usually of little value as a way of promoting your business to new customers.

A better way to get people to talk about your business is to give them a wonderful story to tell. Not a story about the day-to-day running of your business – this is usually quite unexciting to them – but about something completely different. This kind of story will illustrate to potential customers that yours is a business that is quite extraordinary.

Step 3: Creating Super CNe's

Choose something really visible.

Make your Super-CNe's obvious and readily visible. Make sure you can show off your Super-CNe's to your clients so that you receive the benefit of your effort. When you give people something unusual to see, you give them something exciting to talk about.

Dental Buns

> About twelve years ago we decided we'd bake 'Dental Buns' for our customers. I wanted to be able to give them something nice to eat which contained no added sugar — in part to demonstrate how good something could taste and yet not be damaging to teeth. But needless to say my main reason for going to all this trouble was to give my customers something interesting to talk about.
>
> By the time I first designed my new building, I had already decided that baking the Dental Buns was an important part of our day's work. So I built the surgery around a kitchen, away from the customers but close to our main work area. Then it would be easy for us to keep an eye on the buns as they cooked.
>
> Unfortunately, because the customers did not see us cooking the buns, they assumed that we just bought them in from a bakery. This wasn't such an exciting story for them to tell!
>
> So I decided that if we were going to all this trouble, we might as well make a show of it. With this in mind we purchased a little convection oven with all glass sides so you could see what was baking, and we moved the oven out near the Cappuccino Machine, close to the front entrance. It was now obvious to everyone that we were cooking the buns in-house!
>
> There was an immediate increase in interest from our customers. They began to stop for a look when passing the oven — they'd take a good look inside and inhale the aroma. They could actually see the very buns cooking

141

that they would take home at the end of their visit — the same buns they would share with their friends and family.

This Super-CNe became more powerful by becoming more visible. I have noted a similar situation with our espresso machine.

Cappuccino Evolution

A few years ago I was looking at a picture of one of the World Fairs (Milan, I think) from near the turn of the century. The picture showed a cappuccino machine — a magnificent creation with all copper pipes and gauges and a great big boiler on the top!

I resolved to make my cappuccino machine equally as magnificent. I managed to find a large old dummy- boiler to sit on the top of the current machine. I added a few pipes and gauges and had the whole lot — existing machine and all — heavily copper plated. To top it all off, I affixed a large copper-plated eagle to the crest of the boiler, where, with wings outspread, it put the finishing touch to the machine's brooding magnificence.

Now people just can't miss my Cappuccino-Super-CNe. And since all the structural changes the frequency of customer comments has increased. Sometimes it is only a puzzled, "How interesting". But more often it's something positive like, "Wow!" or "Awesome!". Especially from customers who remember the old machine.

It does seem a little strange to me that the coffee even tastes better now — at least that's what my long-standing customers report. Oh, the power of appearance!

Step 4: Creating Super CNe's

Pick an area of customer concern.

142

Hierarchy of Horrors

Mike Basch, famous as a co-founder of FedEx, describes industries as having a 'Hierarchy of Horrors' — a list of fears and frustrations commonly experienced by customers dealing with businesses in their industry. In his books and seminars Mike has described how I managed to address many of these fears and frustrations common to dentistry. While his words are flattering, I can't admit to making these changes with his 'Horrible Hierarchy' in mind — it was not such a deliberate exercise for me.

However, I can definitely say that you should focus your Super-CNe's power on problems that your customers associate with your type of industry. Super-CNe's are most useful when they dispel worries that are likely to upset your customers. And they'll do that *before* a severe lack of trust has time to develop.

Lack of trust was especially endemic in the automobile industry before the recent advancements in manufacturing improved the quality of their products.

In the early days of automobiles, the Rolls Royce Car Company made cars of great quality. One of their sales slogans was, "Rolls Royce motor cars do not break down".

In the twenties (the early days of the motor industry), most cars did break down, very frequently, and there were few auto repair shops.

Engineering was not as advanced as it is now, and most drivers had to be part-time mechanics. So it was very persuasive to say that a Rolls Royce would never need repair on the open road.

To would-be automobile buyers, this marketing angle was probably responsible for many people parting with the large amount of money needed to purchase a 'Rolls'.

I remember hearing a story from that time.

Rolls Break-Down

It happened that a gentleman of greater riches than average but little mechanical ability took his Rolls-Royce car from England to the continent.

In those days this was a journey that one would take with some trepidation. Automobiles were fragile things, and few spares were available in foreign climes. Nevertheless the gentleman had faith in the Rolls slogan and he travelled with his car on the Cross-Channel Ferry to Le Havre.

He motored pleasantly through France for a few days and then crossed into Belgium and then Holland where, on a particularly stony piece of road, the rear axle of his car broke.

The gentleman checked into a local hotel and left his car at the side of the road. From the hotel he telephoned the Rolls Royce Company in England and berated them for not living up to their advertising.

The Rolls employee at the other end listened sympathetically and suggested that the gentleman get a good night's sleep in the hotel, and that he would arrange for the car to be looked at forthwith.

In the morning soon after he arose, the gentleman found himself looking down from the hotel window at his car and wondering how long he would be stranded. As he gazed forlornly at the vehicle, he glimpsed a piece of paper attached to the windshield. He hurried down and found it was a note from a Rolls Royce mechanic. It read:

"I have checked your car, and it is in excellent repair. This is as one would expect because *Rolls Royce motor cars do not break down.* Have a pleasant journey."

At first the gentleman was bemused. After a few moments he realised what must have happened, and he returned to the hotel to collect his luggage, chuckling to himself.

The gentleman continued on his tour of the continent secure in the knowledge that even if he did not have an unbreakable automobile — which would be very impressive — he was watched over by a company that would do anything to maintain the <u>illusion</u> that he had such a vehicle ... and that was even more impressive.

As you might have gathered by now, Rolls Royce had pulled out all the stops to keep its reputation. To keep true to the advertising that Rolls produced unbreakable automobiles, the company had dispatched a mechanic with a new axle on the fast cross-channel steamer. He had fitted it during the night and had left the note as per his instructions.

One of the chief customer concerns at the time of this incident was breakdown. Rolls Royce addressed this concern in a truly memorable way.

Here you see a great example of a Super-CNe, one that produced a story that would be told and retold for more than fifty years. At each telling I am sure it becomes more outrageous. And surely that is one of the strengths of great Super-CNe's. They lend themselves to story telling, and when a positive story is told it tends to become more positive with each re-telling.

Step 5: Creating Super CNe's

Choose something that appears difficult — but really isn't.

It should be obvious to your customers that you have taken great care creating and implementing your Super-CNe's.

Many of the things we do every day in business, when you look at them closely, can easily be made into routine systems. In fact, as a general rule of human nature, the more regularly you perform certain tasks, the simpler and the more systematised they become.

145

But you must make sure that your Super-CNe's always appear as though someone has taken considerable time and care with them. Systematise well, but resist the temptation of simplifying your Super-CNe's so much that your effort becomes invisible in your customers eyes.

Dental Buns Revisited

My daughter, Kate, is a great cook, and when we first thought of making the Dental Buns, she worked hard to produce all sorts of delicious recipes for us. Some recipes were successful, some not so. We vigilantly taste-tested them all!

In fact we tested them so assiduously that our waistlines started to bulge! At this point — or a little beyond this point if I am to be quite truthful — we decided that it would be better for everyone if the buns were also low in calories.

So over the next few months Kate devised six or seven delicious recipes that also had very little fat. Kate started baking them for our clients on a daily basis. We were all quite pleased with this arrangement, but that's just when our difficulties started! Kate left us to start in a new and exciting profession.

When Kate was doing the cooking it was not a lot of hassle for us. But when we had to do it for ourselves — three or four batches each day — it was an enormous amount of extra work. Just making up the batches of mixture took at least an hour.

So we set about simplifying the routine.

We settled on the three most popular recipes and out-sourced the production of the mixture. Hamish, one of our clients who runs a bakery, now delivers a couple of months supply of mixture in plastic food containers. We store them in a freezer, and every afternoon we put two small containers into the fridge to defrost overnight. When we are close to running out of mixture, we just ring Hamish for more.

We used to place the mixture in the baking trays with a special measurer that ensured uniformity of size. Now instead of metal trays, we have paper and foil moulds so there is no cleaning up.

A timer sounds when the buns are cooked and cooled and the Care Nurses load them into the bags under the watchful eyes of the customer. This is the most labour intensive part. Hence this is the part that we want the customers to see.

Our customers can't miss the buns cooking and note the fact that we pack them in specially labelled brown bags. We seal the bags with a ribbon and a card which describes the fact that they are low calorie and contain no added sugar.

I am sure that it seems to people that we go to an extraordinary amount of trouble but they don't realise that everything is systematised.

Step 6: Creating Super CNe's

Take your Super-CNe's to the extreme.

No matter how well you follow the other Super-CNe principles, if you don't do your Super-CNe's to the n'th degree, their effect as a marketing tool will be minimal.

Ordinary Hotel Apples

Recently I stayed in a small boutique hotel that was very cosy and well appointed. The first thing I noticed was the apples on the front desk. What a nice touch, I thought. Is this going to be a Super-CNe? Are they going to make a big thing about apples?

I waited for the receptionist to make some reference to the apples – that they were placed on the counter especially for hotel guests. Unfortunately, I was left wanting. Nothing was said.

The apples looked delicious, and I was tempted to take one anyway. If it had been a big hotel, I would have picked one without a second thought. But I was too embarrassed to do so here because it was not obvious that they were for public consumption (as I later learned they were). It was a small desk with only one receptionist – perhaps they were hers?

During the period I was staying at the hotel, I noticed that no other guest took an apple, either. At the end of the day the bowl was still full of the same apples. The apples were always fresh each day so someone was taking the effort to replace the old ones. But all their effort had gone to waste because they hadn't thought through their system more carefully.

How sad! If only they had taken things further, they could have had a great Super-CNe working for their hotel. If they had only thought a bit more carefully, perhaps they could have provided:

- A small sign suggesting guests should feel free to take an apple from the desk.

- Special types of apples that were not usually sold.

- Apples in the hotel rooms.

- An 'Apple Week' when they offered their guests complimentary apple cider and apple juice and the chance to win a trip to the 'Apple Isle' – Tasmania.

But they didn't, and so the apples on the desk remained uneaten and un-talked about. The thoughtful people at this cosy little hotel are probably discouraged that no one took any of their apples, and I wouldn't be surprised to hear that they have given it up as a bad idea!

Airlines and Their Nuts

There is an Airline in the US that has done away with in-flight meals and offers packets of peanuts instead. I have heard that they are a great airline and memorable for many fun reasons. However, just giving peanuts to passengers can appear a bit 'mean'. I think that with a little change they could turn what seems like parsimony into something memorable and newsworthy. For instance:

Nuts about Nuts – A 'What if' Story

Say you are the CEO of an airline. You have the idea that you want to do away with in-flight meals. You want to be the 'airline that serves peanuts'.

Many people disparage your plans because they feel that to your customers the usual packet of airline peanuts will not be a very satisfactory substitute for an in-flight meal. However, you decide that you are going to do this whole peanut theme to the n'th degree and make the idea work amazingly well.

A few months later customers are getting the full 'peanut experience'.

The first thing that hits them as they walk onto the plane is the aroma ... the delicious smell of fresh roasted nuts.

During each flight the 'Keepers of the Nuts' serves the finest peanuts slowly basted and carried in special peanut carts.

As the 'Keeper' rolls the cart through the cabin, salivating travellers are tempted by the smell of the nuts and the special dipping sauces simmering in the copper receptacles at the side of the cart.

The nuts are dipped in a sauce, placed lovingly into custom made brown paper bags with a pinch of salt in a twist of blue paper and finally served to each passenger with silver tongs on a silver tray.

Customers can read the story of this golden aristocracy of peanuts on the brown paper packaging — how they were tenderly shelled by dusky virgins in the Senegal and flown in on specially chartered planes ... etc, etc.

So what do you think the travellers on this imaginary airline will talk about when they get to their destination?

Scoring Your Super-CNe's

How do you go about rating Super-CNe's? Well, you can do this by seeing how well they follow the *Steps*.

Remember the story about the Rolls Royce motor car that 'never breaks down'? Consider that Super-CNe:

Rolls Rating

1. *Choose an area of interest that you really enjoy.* I would imagine that the mechanics who did the repairs enjoyed the travel and liked taking part in this fun little game. ✓

2. *Choose an area that is distant (but not too distant) from the core of your business.* The elaborate charade took place far from the workshop and was exciting for the owner of the car and for the mechanic. At the same time it demonstrated that Rolls Royce would always maintain its standard of excellence. ✓

3. *Choose something really visible.* The actual events were fairly low key, but their effect was quite observable. I imagine the owner showed the note around to his friends and told the story with gusto. ✓

4. *Choose an area of customer concern.* Yes, breakdowns were of definite concern to Roll's customers in the 20's, and probably it was a great selling point for an automobile company to have an unbreakable product. This is probably the best point of this Super-CNe. ✓

5. *Choose something that appears difficult – but really isn't.* Certainly in the 1920's, considering the transport available at the time, this level of service would have seemed quite arduous. Unfortunately, it really was almost as difficult as it appeared. ✓

6. *Take your Super-CNe to the extreme.* I can't think of a way that Rolls Royce could have gone further or done any better. ✓

Overall, I would give this Super-CNe a nine out of ten!

Another example for rating is a Super-CNe I created for a friend of mine. Here is the process we went through so that you get an idea of how you might make one for yourself.

Jim's Photos

My friend, Jim, runs a bicycle-parts business. He wanted to make his business more exciting for his customers and he wanted to bring them closer to his team.

Some customers had very little contact with his business, and he believed they felt a bit isolated. Jim also wanted his customers to talk about his business (to bicycle owners and other merchants) in glowing terms.

I suggested that Jim make a Super-CNe to achieve these aims, and I went about creating one for him.

Jim is a photography buff. To a certain extent his penchant has rubbed off on the people that work with him, so, using the Super-CNe program steps, I suggested the following:

1) Purchase a digital camera. 2) Each day have someone take a dozen or so snapshots of the activity around the office. 3) Title the photos and print them out in black and white on the laser printer. 4) Send the photos out with each delivery of goods.

"OK," said Jim. "But it's too hard." (In other words it violates the Super-CNe creation Step #5.) So I came up with a modification:

Use a regular camera to take photos around the office. Pick five and have them duplicated in quantity. It may take a week for them to come back so they would be of the previous week, but that's not really important. Send a photo out in each parcel as suggested earlier.

Jim seemed happier with that so we'll see how it goes.

So how did it rate? Well, look at the Super-CNe principles:

1. **[Enjoyable!]** Well, I already knew that they enjoyed the photography.

2. **[Non-Core!]** Photography was distant from the core of Jim's business so that customers would feel his Super-CNe was 'beyond the call of duty'. However if the photos were taken carefully and creatively customers might well assume that this same creativity and attention-to-detail existed in the main part of Jim's business.

3. **[Visible!]** This would be something really visible. Every time a customer opened a package they would see something quite unusual.

4. **[Customer Concern!]** The system addressed was an area of customer concerns: lack of contact.

5. **[Appears difficult!]** The Super-CNe appeared to be difficult but with systematisation it really wasn't that hard once everything was set up.

6. **[Extreme!]** It was taken to the extreme. Who else would send out a photo in a parcel? A team-photo at Christmas? Perhaps. A photo in a newsletter? Yes. But in every parcel? And every week? Now that's taking things to the extreme!

Super-CNe Synergy

Multiply your Super-CNe's power by giving them harmony.

SUPER-CNE SYNERGY

Multiply your Super-CNe's power by giving them harmony.

roperly instructed, Super-CNe's can work together to make the story that they tell far more powerful than it would be if they were working separately.

When Super CNe's work together for a common cause, they are like the heroes in an old tale standing shoulder to shoulder, triumphant over a much larger foe. And like such heroes they can create an overwhelming force: an irresistible story for people to tell about your business.

Super CNe Synergy

The Inventor's Super-CNe's soon started to demonstrate their usefulness. They took some of the areas in which the Inventor was most interested and worked on a system to create a great story for the Inventor's customers to tell.

All on its own, one of the CNe's started organising and managing the others. "What a strange mutation", muttered the Inventor and promptly named it the 'Synergy-CNe' for the way that it pulled all the other Super-CNe's together.

The newly named Synergy-CNe (SS to his friends) took the Inventor's love of Grendling and organised various Super-CNe's to work on a project together.

One Super-CNe made a picture gallery of all the Inventor's Grendling triumphs, and put them in the front office. One took old Grendling tools and placed them in glass fronted cases on the walls. Another made a beautifully bound diary describing in detail the Grendling expeditions the inventor had been on.

Customers who enjoyed grendling — and there were many of them because it was a popular pastime in the kingdom — were fascinated by the display and enjoyed talking to the inventor about his successes and failures.

These customers told other customers about the strange inventor who was an accomplished Grendler and had put so much attention to detail in his exhibition.

As a result of all his Synergy-CNe's hard work the Inventor's business had a noticeable jump in prosperity!

Super-CNe Synergy

Synergy Illuminated

Even though the energy they contain is equal, there is a great difference in the power of a laser and that of a beam of light.

The difference in power lies in the synergy of the beam. The particles of light in the laser are all vibrating in the same direction – with synergy. In the regular beam of light they vibrate randomly. It is because the photons are all working together that the laser is so powerful.

Consider synergy when you make your Super-CNe's. You will create a very powerful story if you make a number of them that follow the same theme.

For instance, if you had a pizza restaurant you might be able to synergise your Super-CNe's by playing old Italian pop songs, having Italian travel books on the tables and naming your dishes after Italian soccer stars.

But do remember that Super-CNe's have to be done to the n'th degree.

- Not just two or three travel magazines about Europe and Italy, but lots of picture books about Italy, old Michelin guides to accommodation and books about the joys of regional Italian cookery!

- Not just a couple of tapes of Italian songs but a whole collection of 78's from the Italian greats of the 1950's played on an old fashioned electric record player.

- Not just the names of the soccer stars on the menu but a picture and biography of each one at the back of the menu together with their scoring statistics over the years.

Together these CNe's would work together to give your customers a far more exciting story to tell about your business than if they were unrelated in theme.

If you consistently follow the rules for creating Super-CNe's and then you make sure that they are all pulling together you will be amazed how effective they can be.

SYNERGISING SUPER-CNE'S INCREASES THEIR EFFECT EXPONENTIALLY.

Story-to-tell Business

When you manage to synergise your Super-CNe's the story that they produce is overwhelming. I think of such enterprises as *Story-to-Tell* businesses.

I play a game with myself to spot potential Super-CNe's in other peoples businesses and imagine how I could build on a theme — to make them all work synergistically — to create a *Story-to-Tell* business.

For example: I was sitting in a new coffee place in a local shopping centre having my usual double decaf skinny-chino when I noticed their logo on the sign above the counter.

Out of Africa

This logo was a carefully designed, stylised giraffe. It was beautiful. Someone had paid a lot of money for that sign!

The giraffe appeared on the sign and place mats, but look as I may, I could find no other visual or written reference to giraffes or Africa in the menu or décor.

The décor was tasteful, chocolate and beige, and the theme was 'earthy', perhaps slightly tropical-Italian. Unfortunately that was it. Apart from the colour scheme there seemed to be no uniting elements.

The coffee was good, but not good enough to rave over. The service was pleasant and timely. But I had no story to tell my friends about my experience other than, "There is a pretty reasonable coffee shop with a nice giraffe sign that has opened over in the shopping centre." Not really a conversation stopper. I felt strangely cheated because I could imagine a far more exciting story that would impress my friends about how I had found this amazing coffee shop ...

My mind wandered and I imagined a place where the theme was Africa:

Staff in uniforms with tiger skin collars,

Instead of saying, "Sir," they would use, "Bwana,"

African rock music playing in the background,

Tables and chairs upholstered with mock leopard skins,

The current minimalist counter disguised with bundles of sticks and dried gourds,

And everywhere would be the giraffe logo!

It wouldn't take much, and I would have had a great story to tell my friends — the owners of that coffee lounge would have had a great *Story-to-Tell* business that their customers would rave over.

Synergy and Theme

One way to produce the synergy that one needs for a *Story-to-Tell* business is to think of it as creating a theme that your Super CNe's all follow.

I once overheard a portion of a story about an American hotel which struck me as having a very definite theme — ducks!

The story has stuck in my mind ever since, and gradually I have added details from my imagination.

I find now that the real story is quite well known. However, I think my tale illustrates the principles of Super-CNe's well, so I hope you forgive me the lack of accuracy.

The Hotel de Duck

There was a hotel that had a flock of ducks land on its roof. The person who maintained the gardens on the roof saw the ducks, and being a lover of wild things, he fed them a couple of times thinking to give them a brief respite on their long trip south. Knowing a good thing when they saw it — room service, hot and cold running water, protection from predators and a great address — the ducks stuck around.

Pretty soon other people who worked in the hotel learned about the ducks and visited them in their rooftop duck-paradise. These people, too, were aficionados of the wild and pampered the ducks with more attention.

The manager of this excellent and ecologically minded hotel eventually heard about the ducky goings-on, and he too, went to the rooftop garden to see for himself what was happening. Well, one look at the ducks and he fell victim to their avian charms!

Now this particular manager was a marketer at heart and could see that, if so many of his employees liked the idea of a group of wild ducks living in the hotel, his patrons might too. And perhaps they might talk persuasively about his duck-friendly hotel to other potential customers. These customers, carrying bags of worms that they had purchased in the special duck-lovers shop set up in the foyer, would also stay at the hotel, use lots of room service and visit the rooftop *Duckery*.

The manager's wild idea blossomed and took shape. As time went on, the ducks became a great attraction. Every day they were escorted from the roof, down in the hotel elevator, across the lobby to the fountain in the foyer. Guests would congregate in the lobby to watch this strange procession of gaily flapping ducks led by the rooftop gardener who had been exotically uniformed and renamed, 'Keeper of the Ducks'.

The ducks, quacking and dabbling and generally being as entertaining as only ducks can be, stayed in the pool all day. In the evening they were led back upstairs by the 'Keeper of the Ducks' under the admiring eyes of hotel guests to take their well earned rest.

The ducks became an institution and the hotel became more and more popular. When the guests returned to their respective homes, they regaled their friends with the story of the 'hotel with the amazing ducks'.

The manager was promoted, and the ducks bred happily (and had to be surreptitiously culled each Christmas!).

My editor knew a little more of the real 'Duck Story' than I. Here is some information that he recommended I include to avoid offending the hotel.

- The Hotel with the ducks is the Peabody Hotel, just off Beale Street in Memphis.

- The Manager was not promoted, and the ducks are not seasonally culled.

- There is no 'duck boutique' in the foyer of the Peabody.

However, the Peabody makes still more of a fuss of their ducks than the hotel I described in my story.

Their ducks have an elaborate mansion-façade to their duck-house on the roof, and they walk grandly through the foyer on a specially coloured carpet (for obvious reasons, if you have ever tried to escort a flock of ducks through a finely appointed public foyer!).

So yet again, fact is proved to be even stranger than fiction. The ducks 'rule' and an awesome *Story-to-Tell* business is alive and well in Memphis, Tennessee.

FATAL FLAW

CNe's have a vital factor that is all
too easy to miss.

Fatal Flaw

---

*CNe's have a vital factor that is all too
easy to miss.*

When a program malfunctions after running well for some time the programmers that I know are prone to joke with each other that the problem is caused by 'software decay'.

This degeneration, they assert to anyone gullible enough to believe them, is caused by gradual deterioration of the stored 1's and 0's in the computer memory.

Now this is a fanciful idea, as they well know, but it takes some of the sting out of the bad feeling they get when one of their programs is found to have a 'bug' (read 'mistake') in the code — the real reason for the malfunction.

In the real world, however, decay of systems is an ever present problem. Human beings are not as consistent as computer devices and they do make little changes to the way things are done. Over time these small changes add up, and they become the new norm.

Fatal Flaw

Things were going very well for the Inventor. He had lots of customers, thanks to his Super-CNe's and because of his CNe's, his customers believed he was the greatest inventor in the world. Business was thriving!

Unfortunately, it was not to stay that way. The Inventor started to notice little signs that all was not well with his CNe's. He saw dust left in the corner of the laboratory, a few instruments not put away and CNe's chatting in a corner when they should have been out working.

After a few days, the CNe's slackened off a little more and the laboratory was starting to degenerate into its old untidy state. Pretty soon his customers started to grumble about similar problems with their CNe's.

The CNe's were changing back into the horrid Ne's!

Just when things were going really well for the kingdom, it was becoming obvious that the Inventor was not as good as he seemed to be. The people started to mutter angry words about the Inventor and the CNe's-turned-Ne's were starting to hang around on street corners again ...

Fatal Flaw

I made lots of CNe's and a few Super-CNe's and they worked very well. I even felt confident enough to advise other people on the creation of CNe's for their businesses. I believed that I had discovered everything there was to know about the subject.

I felt a little smug when I saw that others did not understand how truly useful CNe's could be in business ... or how to make them for themselves – I feel about the CNe's somewhat as Albert Einstein did about the magic of compounding interest!

However, I did feel a small sense of disquiet when some of the systems I had so carefully set up occasionally went wrong.

The ones that failed weren't actually my CNe or Super-CNe systems. But if some of my regular systems were malfunctioning, perhaps my CNe's were not immune?

Take the case of the system surrounding one of our important pieces of heavy equipment.

The Compressor

> The air compressor in a dental business is vitally important because almost all of the small dental tools run on compressed air from this machine.
>
> Customers don't actually see the compressor, but, if it's not working well, they hear it. They notice when we have to blow their teeth a little more because of water in the line, or when the air smells a bit oily.
>
> The compressor needs to be reliable, and we had a system taking special care of it. I documented the system and had a checklist.

In our previous building we'd had to drain the compressor by hand. It was an arduous task, but it was always done.

In the new building I installed a remote drain that required only a simple turn of a tap rather than crawling around the machine. It was far easier so I didn't think about changing the checklist.

One day the compressor ground to a smoking halt: full of water. It didn't take long to find out what had happened, but it did take a few days to repair the problem and that disrupted our work considerably.

Because it was not on the old checklist and the new tap was not marked, after a while everyone forgot it was there. And because there was no drain tap on the compressor itself, everyone had assumed that it drained automatically. The build up of water caused an overload on the motor, and it stopped working!

It was annoying that the compressor had broken down. It caused so much trouble. Even more importantly, one of our carefully created systems had failed … and that was very scary! And the compressor maintenance system was not the only one that gave trouble.

Gas Attack

We had a system for ordering the cylinders of oxygen that we use for sedation and emergency resuscitation. As you can imagine, it is very important that one can rely on oxygen being available exactly when it is needed. The system was well thought out, and I considered it foolproof. Well, foolproof it was, but not impervious to systems-decay!

One day I turned on the tap to give a patient some oxygen before I gave them some anaesthetic gas. Nothing happened. No reassuring rush of life giving gas from the mask, no steady inflation of the black rubber bag, nothing, zilch!

I apologised to the patient and abandoned the procedure.

It was really lucky this was not an emergency and I was depending on the gas for revival of an oxygen starved unfortunate.

Somehow our infallible system malfunctioned and the gas wasn't ordered. When I investigated, I found that the gas checking system we were using had been subtly altered from our original creation. The system then no longer reliably indicated when gas was needed! Horror!

This is an example of creeping systems decay. It is important to be ever vigilant to prevent the problems it causes. I had not been vigilant enough, thus the scary situation when the system had changed and I had no emergency oxygen.

BUSINESS SYSTEMS NEED UPGRADING TO CHANGE WITH THE TIMES.

All of this systems breakdown was bad enough, but one day there was another failure, and this time it was a very important Super-CNe, our flagship, my beloved cappuccino machine.

The Cappuccino Machine (Revisited)

It became apparent that our coffee was not up to scratch!

It did not taste as good as it usually did. Customers were starting to become less effusive in their praise of our cappuccinos and lattés, and there were little black bits that didn't look like coffee grains in the bottom of the cups when they had finished.

We finally traced the problem to the boiler in the cappuccino machine.

It had become full of black rust. The seals on the valves operated by my favourite large chrome handles had perished, and the filter had become clogged. The net effect was nasty looking bits in the water.

168

We called the supplier's repair men to the task, and as it turns out, not only did they prevent a few more problems that were waiting to happen, but they also put me onto the folks who had the large old dummy-domed boiler that I had copper plated and which now sits on the top of my machine to make it look even more magnificent than it did before.

Problem solved, system improved, Super-CNe back on track!

So, we had found a solution pretty quickly, but it worried me that we had come to this. How could we stop it happening in the future? Surely there must be an answer ...

FINAL CHALLENGE

Keeping your CNe's healthy.

FINAL CHALLENGE

Keeping your CNe's healthy.

s time goes by there is a tendency for systems to deteriorate. This gradual breakdown of systems is called *systems-decay* and is caused by a progressive accumulation of small errors and changes made by those using the system.

Sometimes people leave steps out, change some detail or do others inadequately. If these changes are not seen or addressed, they become entrenched.

When the system is then taught to another person, the modifications are passed on. If you have a high turnover of the people using the system, this effect is even more pronounced.

Documentation can help but even documentation can be ignored or misinterpreted. No matter how well a system works, it is of little worth unless it is used and unless it produces the result for which it was designed.

As time passes, even when the system works exactly as it is written, because circumstances for which it was designed have changed the results may be not what was intended.

CNe's are basically systems, and all CNe's eventually fail in one way or another. It is difficult to make a good CNe and sad to let it decay simply because there is not a way to keep it up to scratch.

So, to have good long-term results, it is not enough just to create CNe's. You also need to have a method of keeping your CNe's in tune.

The Final Challenge

The poor Inventor, afraid to go out for fear of the angry villagers, sat in his little laboratory and watched all his hard work go down the drain as the CNe's gradually deteriorated.

His wonderful helpers were changing back in to the lazy, degenerate Ne's. Already they were doing almost no work at all — their appearance was becoming tattier by the hour!

What could have gone wrong?

In the midst of his despair, the Inventor remembered that there was one document that remained in the box left to him by his grandfather. Previously he had put this paper aside as just too hard to translate. Now, hoping it held the solution to his problem, he set to work to interpret it.

Once again the lights in the little laboratory could be seen burning in the small hours of the morning as the Inventor struggled with the archaic words and type.

When his work was completed, he understood the significance of the Master Inventor's final discovery about the CNe's. It was so obvious. All things undergo change, systems become corrupted, and CNe's are no exception: they need regular upkeep and care.

Now it all made sense. "So that's why CNe's degenerated after the Master Inventor was banished. When he was no longer around to maintain them the CNe's gradually deteriorated into Ne's."

With rising anticipation, the Inventor reprogrammed the Generator, collared a reluctant Ne, stuffed it into the central chamber, and pulled down on the main power switch.

There was the usual pyrotechnic display before the conveyor clacked into life and deposited the little being onto the floor. With a sigh of relief the Inventor watched the newly regenerated CNe pick up a broom and go about its work!

Over the next few days the Inventor reprogrammed all of the Ne's, and, if anything, they were better than before.

They set to work again willingly and now, because of an extra part in their programming, they also filled out Report Cards. From these reports the Inventor was able to tell when his CNe's were starting to deteriorate, and to take appropriate reprogramming action.

With the final pieces of the CNe system in place the Inventor's business quickly regained its old efficiency. First the people in the village, and then all the people of the kingdom, brought their CNe's back to be refreshed.

Once again the Inventor's expertise was celebrated throughout the land.

Final challenge

On Systems

Up until my problems with the CNe's degenerating, I believed that the essence of a good system was that:

- It was well documented and described in easy to understand steps.

- It was obvious who was responsible for modifying the system.

- It was easily performed.

- It had an outcome that was obvious and measurable.

- It had a simple checklist.

All of these factors certainly are important, but there were two even more vital factors missing from my list.

It took me far too long to discover just what they were:

- Have a simple, easily checked method of reporting.

- Make sure you do regular reprogramming.

Reporting on Systems

Without a report you can spend lots of time and effort making a great system to do the tasks around your business, only to notice a few months later that the job you so carefully systematised is not being done or is being done incorrectly. It's happened to me, and I am sure it has happened to you.

You check with the person who is supposed to be doing the task and they swear they are doing just as they have been shown ... or that they thought the system had been changed ... or they did it differently because it was a waning moon, or a full moon, or Ethiopian Liberation Day ... all sorts of reasons.

Solving this problem of human fallibility necessitates a way of easily checking on the performance of the system.

The mistake I made in creating my original CNe's was that I forgot to build in a reporting function.

This meant that the CNe's started off well but after a few months they started to deteriorate. I assumed they were still going well but I didn't really know whether or not that was the case. Later, I tended to avoid checking up because I had a sneaking suspicion that all was not well, and I didn't want to feel bad about it – typical ostrich management technique. Eventually I had to face the facts.

Reprogramming

You need a reporting function to discover whether your CNe's continue to work well. In fact, the better and more visible the reporting, the longer CNe's seem to work without degeneration.

However, just reporting is not enough. Something needs to be done with the report and when things are no longer going well with a particular CNe, it needs to be altered.

That process is called CNe Reprogramming.

The best reprogramming is done in discussion with those who use the system. This is the method I use:

- Meet together with all the people involved in the CNe.

- Discuss the changes.

- Rewrite the CNe's system.

- Remove all references to the old system and post the new system in a very visible place so everyone is reminded of the changes.

The CNe's have been a great boon to me in my work of creating a happy and successful business. Over time they have become more alive and human to me, and I have learned a lot from their simple wisdom.

The Smiling CNe's

You will notice that in the drawings of the CNe's they are always smiling. The Ne's however, are always frowning. The Ne's don't work; their whole life is a holiday. They do whatever they want. And yet they do not seem happy.

CNe's don't have holidays and they work very long hours and they don't get paid. What they do have is a sense of purpose, a pleasant atmosphere in which to operate and enjoyable outcomes of which they can be proud.

The Master Inventor programmed the CNe's to be happy in their work. As long as they have an efficient and useful way of doing the tasks for which they were designed (and as long as their work is respected by their possessors) they remain joyful.

There is a lesson in that for all of us.

As I mentioned initially, the message of this book is actually quite simple. Let me summarise in a few words what took me decades to understand:

1. Take care of the incidentals (the CNe's) if you want to have people respect your core product or service.

2. Do things that give your customers a great story to tell about your business — the Super CNe's.

And perhaps you won't mind if I now add a third point in keeping with my penchant for a business that brings me great pleasure:

3. If you are going to do something in your business make sure that it gives you as much happiness as possible.

— you deserve it!

I hope I have managed to convince you that my points are valid. I wish you all the best in creating a little army of CNe's in your business that help make your business life more productive and enjoyable.

Paddi Lund

Happy CNe's

Happy
The Inventor
^

At the little laboratory the Inventor now went happily about his business. He was still bearded but both his hair and beard were flecked with white.

Older now, his shoulders were hunched a little, and he had lost some of the spring in his step. But the bright gleam in his eye still persisted.

He still worked at his trade, but his laboratory was quite changed from the cold, disorderly and desolate place it once was. Now it was pristinely clean and tidy, kept so by diminutive CNe's who raced hither and thither making sure that everything was spick-and-span.

In pride of place in the centre of the laboratory, the CNe generator now sparkled from constant polishing.

The Inventor's business was very successful and extremely profitable. New customers came to the Inventor from far and wide. They heard the story of his Super-CNe's and they believed that he must be a great inventor.

He, however, remained humble. He knew that though he was quite good at his job he was not nearly as good as his customers believed. He understood the power of his CNe's to change perceptions, and he knew that without them he would be eating crusts again.

Sometimes in the evening, after they had finished their work, the CNe's and the Inventor would all join hands to dance and sing together while the stars shone down approving light on the little laboratory.

And so for many years in this way the Inventor (and his CNe's) lived happily ever after.

THE END

EPILOGUE

A few years ago Paddi wrote a little business story for Mike Basch, a US business expert and one of the founders of FedEx. It was entitled, "The Secrets of the By-Referral-Only Masters". I have always been intrigued by the eighth secret:

> *The value of thy wares speaketh through your soft carpets and hospitality.*

Now that Paddi has written in detail describing exactly what he meant by this somewhat cryptic verse, you can use the ideas contained in this little book to help you make your business more desirable in the eyes of your customers.

Paddi is quite fond of his CNe's (the *Critical Non-Essentials*®) that are hard at work in his dental practice and specifically the concept itself — it's one of his favourite business ideas. The CNe's and Super CNe's are a prime example of Paddi's unique ability to *think differently* about what it means to be in business.

Systems for CNe's

Mike Basch has a great saying, "Systematise the routine; humanise the exception."

If you can make the every-day things that happen in your business work automatically, then you will have time and energy left for when unusual things need managing. If all of your energy is used up because you continually have to think about things that could be automatic, you lose the opportunity to shine when an unforeseen problem arises.

It is hard to make sure that the little details are always done in a consistent way. And yet it is the little details that make so much difference to your client's perception of your business. And that is where systems come in, systems that can take care of the little details. Certainly, it takes time and effort to make good systems, but it is time and effort that will be well rewarded.

Paddi's CNe's

When you hear the story of Paddi's business (from his customers, readers and business experts around the world), what you invariably learn is that...

- Paddi has no signs on his building, and he's taken his name out of the phone book.

- The front door is locked, and when you ring the bell you're greeted by name by your own CareNurse!

- Paddi has a Cappuccino Machine, over 40 varieties of teas and coffees ... all for his customers delight!

- They serve the tea in Royal Doulton China with an elaborate Tea Ceremony!

- Throughout the day they bake fresh Dental Buns (no sugar, low fat muffins of their own recipe), and if the smell as you walk through the door isn't tempting enough, you can see them baking in a special see-through oven right near the Cappuccino Machine.

- You have your own Personal Lounge with your name and photograph (if it's your second visit) right on the door, and they knock asking permission before they enter!

- On the way to your personal lounge (in your second visit), you notice a large picture album – a customer-family photo album – and you see it has been opened to the page with your picture.

- Before you visit Paddi's practice for the first time you're sent a very large and impressive *Welcome Book* which thoughtfully addresses every concern you might have about coming to a new dentist.

- Each room you see is complimented by modest vases of fresh flowers, which always appear as if they were picked that day.

- Adorning nearly every wall are tasteful original works of art depicting a variety of scenes, all painted by his mother Elizabeth Lund.

- There's a jug of cold water there for you, with a sprig of fresh mint, along with a plate of fresh seasonal and dried fruits and nuts, all presented on the same lovely china service plates with classic white paper doilies.

- For when you're in the dental chair, there's a TV on the ceiling, you're given sunglasses for the bright light, your CareNurse applies cream for your lips so that they don't dry out and become uncomfortable, and you're given a hot, scented towel at the end to refresh yourself.

- If you were to visit the 'Gold Bathroom', you'd see real hand towels, hand crème and an impressive array of French and other exotic perfumes.

- And when it comes time for you to leave, you'll almost never leave empty handed; you'll invariably have a bunch of flowers, a bottle of champagne, a packet of dental buns (for your family or work colleagues – because they will ask) or some other special gift.

All of these CNe's and Super-CNe's make for great stories that really interest and excite the right kind of potential customers (as well as business people alike around the world).

Where to from here

If you would like to see photographs of Paddi's favourite Critical Non-Essentials® in action, as well as more pictures of his dental business, you can do so at...

www.PaddiLund.com

You'll also find a picture tour of Paddi's practice, as well as a rough plan and layout of his building, and even a copy of the *Daily Tasks Checklist*, Paddi's first CNe, which ensures that his practice and service experience run flawlessly every day.

If you've enjoyed this publication of Paddi's, you might also enjoy the other publications in the Paddi Series. You can learn all about them at the website above.

For example, if you haven't already read it, we highly recommend Paddi's first and most popular book, *Building the Happiness-Centred Business*. And Paddi's Super CNe's are a very strong basis for an effective and systematised referral system for your business. In which case, Paddi's *Mobilising Your Customer Sales Force* will tell you all about how Paddi harnesses the power of his customers endorsements to their friends and colleagues.

Remember the 'Little Things'

For many years a prominent Australian breakfast cereal company has advertised one of its older (yet more ordinary and more popular) products with a tag-line of, "The simple things in life are often the best".

Well, according to Dr Paddi Lund and his experiences in a small service business, it's "The Little Things in business are always remembered".

We hope you've enjoyed reading Paddi's tale about the Critical Non-Essentials® and his discovery of their importance and effectiveness in commerce and how people perceive your business.

We also hope you are able to use some of these important principles to help create more memorable customer experiences in your business.

Fletcher Potanin
Publisher
For all at Solutions Press